# OPENING THE WINDOWS OF YOUR SOUL

# OPENING THE WINDOWS OF YOUR SOUL

Discovering the Life-Changing Impact
of the Lord's Prayer

By
James Cantelon

RESOURCE *Publications* • Eugene, Oregon

OPENING THE WINDOWS OF YOUR SOUL
Discovering the Life-Changing Impact of the Lord's Prayer

Copyright © 2024 James Cantelon. All rights reserved. Except for brief quotations in critical publications or reviews, no part of this book may be reproduced in any manner without prior written permission from the publisher. Write: Permissions, Wipf and Stock Publishers, 199 W. 8th Ave., Suite 3, Eugene, OR 97401.

Resource Publications
An Imprint of Wipf and Stock Publishers
199 W. 8th Ave., Suite 3
Eugene, OR 97401

www.wipfandstock.com

PAPERBACK ISBN: 979-8-3852-0548-6
HARDCOVER ISBN: 979-8-3852-0549-3
EBOOK ISBN: 979-8-3852-0550-9

VERSION NUMBER 010524

Scripture quotations marked (NIV) are taken from the Holy Bible, New International Version®, NIV®. Copyright ©1973, 1978, 1984, 2011 by Biblica, Inc.™ Used by permission of Zondervan. All rights reserved worldwide. www.zondervan.com The "NIV" and "New International Version" are trademarks registered in the United States Patent and Trademark Office by Biblica, Inc.™

Scripture quotations marked (KJV) are taken from The Authorized (King James) Version. Rights in the Authorized Version in the United Kingdom are vested in the Crown. Reproduced by permission of the Crown's patentee, Cambridge University Press

Scripture quotations marked (NLT) are taken from the Holy Bible, New Living Translation, copyright ©1996, 2004, 2015 by Tyndale House Foundation. Used by permission of Tyndale House Publishers, Carol Stream, Illinois 60188. All rights reserved.

To Kathy,
for whom and
with whom
I pray every morning.

# Contents

*Preface* | ix
*An Invitation* | xvii
*The Setting* | xix

**The Windows** | 1

Window No. 1: **Identity** | 7

Window No. 2: **Family** | 16

Window No. 3: **Home** | 23

Window No. 4: **Worship** | 31

Window No. 5: **Humility** | 41

Window No. 6: **Accountability** | 49

Window No. 7: **Purpose** | 57

Window No. 8: **Simplicity** | 65

Window No. 9: **Forgiveness** | 70

Window No. 10: **Courage** | 79

Postscript: **David's Prayer** | 89

# Preface

> Be not rash with your mouth, nor let your heart be hasty to utter a word before God, for God is in heaven and you upon earth; therefore let your words be few.
>
> —Eccl 5:2

The book of Genesis tells us that Adam and Eve had direct access to and conversation with God. He would join them "in the garden in the cool of the day" (Gen 3:8) where they would converse person to person. When they sinned they were banished, but not abandoned. After Abel's murder by his brother Cain, Adam and Eve had other children. Over the next several decades, grandchildren, great-grandchildren, nephews, nieces, and cousins all emerged in the extended family. As civilization began to take shape, Genesis tells us that "at that time people began to call on the name of the Lord" (Gen 4:26b). They began to pray.

Prayer was not what it is today. In many ways it was akin to magic. Local deities had to be manipulated via sacrifice, *finessed* with ritual. God (or the gods) was distant. He no longer walked in the garden.

Centuries later, a man named Abram was born in Mesopotamia. Some biblical scholars speculate that he emerged from the polytheism of his world to belief in one God by reasoning back to an uncaused Cause/Creator. Later known as Abraham, he became "the father of the faithful" (Gen 17:1–8). He prayed simple,

## Preface

straightforward prayers (e.g., Gen 15:2–16) and received very straightforward responses from the Lord (e.g., Gen 17:1–22). His prayers are described as "calling on the name of the Lord" and they were often accompanied or followed by the building of altars and making sacrifice (Gen 12:8; 13:4). His son Isaac did likewise (Gen 26:25), as did Israel in succeeding centuries.

Abraham and his descendants had a very *serious* view of God. The Lord had revealed himself to Abram as his "shield" (Gen 15:1) and Abram referred to him as "the Judge of all the earth" (Gen 18:25). He was "the Fear of Isaac" (Gen 31:42) and "the Mighty One of Jacob . . . the Shepherd, the Rock of Israel" (Gen 49:24). God was a God of dread and dangerous (1 Sam 6:19–20; 11:7; 2 Sam 6:6–9), demanding obedience (1 Sam 15:22). He was not to be taken lightly. Prayer must always be from the heart (Hos 7:14), and was predicated on thankfulness for God's gracious acts in history.

Centuries later the prophet Isaiah had a profound encounter with God in the temple. It's a model of transforming prayer (Isa 6):

1. In the year that King Uzziah died, I saw the Lord, high and exalted, seated on a throne; and the train of his robe filled the Temple.

2. Above him were seraphim, each with six wings: with two wings they covered their faces, with two they covered their feet, and with two they were flying.

3. And they were calling to one another: "Holy, holy, holy is the Lord Almighty; the whole earth is full of his glory."

4. At the sound of their voices the doorposts and thresholds shook and the temple was filled with smoke.

5. "Woe to me!" I cried. "I am ruined! For I am a man of unclean lips, and my eyes have seen the king, the Lord Almighty."

6. Then one of the seraphim flew to me with a live coal in his hand, which he had taken with tongs from the altar.

7. With it he touched my mouth and said, "See, this has touched your lips; your guilt is taken away and your sin atoned for!"

8. Then I heard the voice of the Lord saying, "Whom shall I send? And who will go for us?" And I said, "Here am I. Send me!"

9a. He said, "Go and tell this people . . ."

The much loved King Uzziah, after fifty years on the throne, had died of leprosy. The prophet Isaiah had joined the nation in mourning. During the seven days of lamentation Isaiah had a vision as he worshiped the Lord in the temple. Suddenly his worship was interrupted by a vision of God (a *theophany*) on his throne, attended by heavenly attendants. As they cried, "Holy, holy, holy!" the earth shook and the temple was filled with God's presence. Isaiah's reaction was quick; he was overwhelmed with guilt. He cried out in distress, seeing himself as a spiritual leper with "unclean lips." (Uzziah had been isolated in his palace, but common lepers had to cover their mouths when approached by unsuspecting pedestrians and cry, "Unclean! Unclean!") His confession of sin was from the heart. Then one of the seraphim touched his lips with a live coal from the altar and declared him cleansed. Awash in gratitude, Isaiah responded to God's call for a prophet emissary with instant commitment, and he was commissioned to "go and tell this people." The transformative moment had a fascinating progression: worship—theophany—confession—cleansing—commitment—commission. This had been no casual conversation.

Unlike his contemporary Isaiah (who was a courtier), the prophet Amos was a rustic. His skin was toughened and his hands gnarly from shepherding and pruning fruit trees. Yet, he was literate and had a poetic gifting. He may have been the first of the Old Testament prophets to commit his words to writing. To him, prayer was inevitable because meeting God was inevitable: "The Lord roars from Zion and thunders from Jerusalem" (Amos 1:2).

And, because he had chosen Israel (Amos 3:2), the only way to live was to seek the Lord. Indeed, seeking God was seeking good: "Seek good, not evil, that you may live. Then the Lord God Almighty will be with you." (Amos 5:14).

God's choosing of Israel had obliged the nation to covenant, and even though this required a distinct liturgical and religious component it was clear that God wanted prayer to be more than lip service:

> Go to Bethel and sin; Go to Gilgal and sin yet more. Bring your sacrifices every morning, your tithes every three years.
>
> Burn leavened bread as a thank offering and brag about your freewill offerings—boast about them, you Israelites, for this is what you love to do.
>
> (Amos 4:4–5)

> I hate, I despise your religious festivals; your assemblies are a stench to me.
>
> Even though you bring me burnt offerings and grain offerings, I will not accept them. Though you bring choice fellowship offerings, I will have no regard for them.
>
> Away with the noise of your songs! I will not listen to the music of your harps.
>
> But let justice roll on like a river, righteousness like a never-failing stream!
>
> (Amos 5:21–24)

Many other prophets picked up on this theme as well (Isa 1:1–11; Hos 6:6: "For I desire mercy, not sacrifice, and acknowledgment of God rather than burnt offerings"). The prophets echoed a constant theme from heaven: "Return to me." But Israel's recalcitrance had dire consequences (Amos 4):

> 6. I gave you empty stomachs in every city and lack of bread in every town, yet you have not returned to me;
>
> 7. I also withheld rain from you when the harvest was still three months away. I sent rain on one town, but withheld it from another. One field had rain; another had none and dried up.

8. People staggered from town to town for water but did not get enough to drink, yet you have not returned to me;

9. Many times I struck your gardens and vineyards, destroying them with blight and mildew. Locusts devoured your fig and olive trees, yet you have not returned to me;

10. I sent plagues among you as I did to Egypt. I killed your young men with the sword, along with your captured horses. I filled your nostrils with the stench of your camps, yet you have not returned to me;

11. I overthrew some of you as I overthrew Sodom and Gomorrah. You were like a burning stick snatched from the fire, yet you have not returned to me;

12. Therefore this is what I will do to you, Israel, and because I will do this to you, Israel, prepare to meet your God.

Meeting God is inevitable. Meeting him on our terms is perilous. Meeting him on his terms is redemptive. Prayer changes things.

Prayer and the Psalms go hand in hand. For centuries the Psalms have been read, sung, and prayed by the people of God. It's surprising, then, to see that only five of the 150 psalms are specifically called "prayers"; these are Ps 17, Ps 86, Ps 90, Ps 102, and Ps 142. But most of them express praise, confession, trust, petition, intercession, and (on David's part) *much* imprecation. Here is a summary of some of those themes from the book of Psalms:

1. Confession of sin (32; 51, etc.)

2. Cries for help (22; 31; 38, etc.)

3. Declarations of trust (23; 46; 62; 84; 90; 91; 103; 121, etc.)

4. Confidence that God hears prayer (3:4; 4:1; 6:9; 17:6; 65:2; 138:3)

5. Prayers that God will answer (20:5; 54:2; 55:1; 61:1; 71:2; 86:6; 130:2; 143:1)

6. Concern about God's silence (10:1; 13:1–2; 77:5–9; 83:1; 89:46; 109:1, etc.)

7. Rehearsal of divine interventions in history (9:1; 44:1–8; 65:5–12; 68:7–18; 77:11–22; 78; 105; 106; 114)

8. Songs of ascent to Jerusalem (120–134)

9. Imprecatory psalms (68; 109; 5; 6; 11; 12; 35; 37; 137; 139, etc.)

10. Wholehearted prayer (108:1; 111:1)

In every prayer there is hope that God will respond favorably: "I call to you Lord, come quickly to me; hear me when I call to you. May my prayer be set before you like incense; may the lifting up of my hands be like the evening sacrifice" (Ps 141:1–2).

The bottom line is the (correct) assumption that as we approach God, "O Thou that hearest prayer" (Ps 65:2), his "arm . . . is not too short to save, nor his ear too dull to hear" (Isa 59:1). He took the initiative in creation. We are "the work of his hands" (Ps 19:1); "he is not willing that any should perish" (2 Pet 3:9); and he "loves the world" (John 3:16). The awareness of his steadfast love is the basis of all prayer. He has our back.

Indeed he does. He *hears* the cry of a child (Gen 21:17); he *hears* the lament of slaves (Exod 3:7–8); he *invites* the thirsty and hungry to come to him (Isa 55:1); he *employs* his heavenly hosts in supporting his servants: "O Daniel, I have now come out to give you wisdom and understanding" (Dan 9:22); by his Holy Spirit he even *prays* for us (Rom 8:26–27); and he *knows* our need before we ask of him (Matt 6:8). Calling to us from a position of strength, he *invites* us to "draw near" to his glorious holiness and redeeming mercy with contrition, respect, and love. He "rewards them that diligently seek him" (Heb 11:6).

In the four Gospels we see Jesus modeling prayer. You would find it a compelling exercise to read all four, making note of the various circumstances and occasions that precipitated prayer on Jesus' part. At his baptism, in solitary settings (often at night), before preaching tours, interceding for his disciples, giving thanks before working miracles, at the transfiguration, facing crises, even

## Preface

on the cross (!), Jesus prayed. His life and ministry were an ongoing conversation with his Father. The lines of communication, speaking and listening, were always open.

The pivot point of all biblical prayer is Jesus' prayer in Gethsemane (Mark 14:36). "Not my will but thine be done" captures it. Nothing need be added. The problem for us is that our prayers can be self-seeking: "When you ask you do not receive because you ask with wrong motives, that you may spend what you get on your pleasures" (Jas 4:3). We may not say it, we may not even believe it, but we pray as if God is there to serve us. He is our personal household deity.

In the preamble before his teaching on prayer in the Sermon on the Mount, Jesus made a profound point that underscores all prayer (Matt 6):

> 5. And when you pray do not be like the hypocrites, for they love to pray standing in the synagogues and on the street corners to be seen by others. Truly I tell you, they have received their reward in full.
>
> 6. But when you pray, go into your room, close the door and pray to your Father, who is unseen. Then your Father, who sees what is done in secret, will reward you.
>
> 7. And when you pray, do not keep on babbling like pagans, for they think they will be heard because of their many words.
>
> 8. Do not be like them, for your Father knows what you need before you ask him.

The point? Brief, secret prayer gains traction with heaven. Never forget your Father is both omniscient and loving. He *knows* and *acts*. But he rarely provides immediate gratification. He acts with the long-term in view.

When I was five years old the concept of a long-term view hadn't occurred to me. I wanted, and prayed for, a pony *now*. My prayers were fervent and persistent but the Lord let me down. No pony. The feeding, housing, veterinary care, and overall sustainability issues were not in my thinking but they were in his. I can't say I had a crisis of faith over this unanswered prayer but I was disappointed. I didn't realize that "no" is just as much an answer as "yes." "Wait" works too.

The waters would have been muddied for me if I had read one of the myriad books available on *effective prayer* (read: "how to get what you want out of God"). The essential thesis is this: if you know how to convince him, God will give you what you ask. You just need to know the method.

When my three kids were little imagine my chagrin if I had overheard them having a discussion of "how to get what you want out of Dad." The method of approach, the words used, the tone of voice, the facial expression, the emotion . . . all as a means to manipulate me. How sad I would have been. They would not have even thought of the big picture or my vision for their lives. I saw them as future adult friends in process, not demanding consumers. I wanted, and would give, not what they asked but what they needed. And because I loved them a little indulgence along the way would factor in as well.

There are two wills in the prayer equation. Unfortunately, our will is often predominant. We need to learn to let our words be few. It's better to think of prayer as the Lord saying, "I hear you. Now hear me."

# An Invitation

SEVERAL YEARS AGO, ON one of my television shows, I interviewed the Rev. John Stott, for twenty-five years the rector of All Souls Church in London, former chaplain to the Queen, and the author of several best-selling books. For two hours we talked about his life, faith, and ministry. At one point I asked this question: "Dr. Stott, how do you start your day?"

> [JS] Well, first of all, I get out of bed slowly. I've got an inner ear problem that sees me falling to the ground if I move too quickly. I stretch. Then I pray the Lord's Prayer. I find it covers the bases. If there's something that was pressing before the Prayer, it seems to lose clout as I pray. If it lingers, I might breathe a word or two about it afterwards, but usually the Prayer is all I need. It sets me up for the day. I can spend the rest of it just listening. Oh yes, I almost forgot—after praying the Prayer I pronounce the Gloria.
>
> [ME] The Gloria?
>
> [JS] Yes. You know. "Glory to the Father, Glory to the Son, Glory to the Spirit, as it was in the beginning so shall it ever be, world without end." I find that the first thing I get in the morning is perspective. I'm a small, bit player in a large, unfolding drama. The Prayer says it all.

As Dr. Stott spoke, I recalled the early morning deliveries of the *Globe and Mail* newspaper I used to make as a kid, the heavy newspaper bag thumping against my thigh as I walked, my only companions the early birds and an occasional neighborhood dog.

## An Invitation

I remembered getting back home, especially in the dark of the northern Ontario winter mornings, putting some water on to boil for my morning oatmeal, and then, even while my mother and siblings still slept (my dad already in the basement for early morning prayer), opening the window blinds of our home to the first rays of the morning light. It struck me one subzero February morning, the muted sounds of my Dad's praying below me, that even the entry of a dawning early light quietly filling a room was rather like prayer—one opened the windows of one's soul, as it were, when one prayed. Maybe this was why my dad's face seemed to shine every morning when he emerged from the basement, his Bible and a cup of coffee in hand.

Now, forty years later, with the man Billy Graham called the most influential pastor of the twentieth century across from me, his face shining with a kind of preternatural light, I think, "He's right! The Lord's Prayer does cover everything. I'm going to start every day with this Prayer. What's more, I'm going to study it in depth. Maybe it's the key to 'opening the windows of my soul.'"

So, I followed through, and this book chronicles the journey. I say *journey*, because it is. What I've written is only a description of what I've discovered so far. But, for me, the Prayer has had, is having, and will continue to have a huge impact on my life. I've identified ten *windows* the Prayer opens—windows that let the early morning light and the freshest of air into the *room* of my soul. I'd like to invite you, the reader, to join me.

Let's let the light shine in.

# The Setting

IT WAS LATE AFTERNOON, in April 1982. I was returning to Jerusalem from southern Lebanon, where I had done two shifts broadcasting from a radio station located in the Valley of the Springs, a battlefield just below Beaufort Castle. That old crusader castle had been a focal point of an ongoing conflict between the Israeli army and the Palestine Liberation Organization (PLO), and my ears were still ringing with the ripping explosions of Katyusha rockets, the deep-throated popping of mortar shells, the earth-shaking, soul-squashing thunder of artillery fire, and the steady staccato of tank and anti-tank battle. My eyes could still see the otherworldly, piercing brightness of last night's parachute flares descending eerily and gracefully from the sky to the battle below. And I could smell the lingering odors of the spent explosives and smoke of countless fires. I was reeling, to say the least, too dazed to appreciate the peace and beauty of the Upper Galilee as I drove south.

Just past Rosh Pinna the highway began its descent to the Sea of Galilee. As this iconic sea came into view hundreds of feet below, I suddenly awoke from my battle haze to the stunning scene before me.

It was as though I were descending an alpine slope on skis. Instead of snow, intensely green grass exploded in the exuberance of spring, painted a heavenly color by the slanting rays of the setting sun. The mountain tops on either side were crowned with the ancient homes of the mystical town of Safat on my right and the

## The Setting

modern *kibbutzim* of Israel on the Golan Heights to my left. Between these vigilant guardians the road twisted and turned, down, down, past biblical Chorazim, through outcroppings of volcanic rock, flocks of brilliantly white sheep grazing on the grass growing between the boulders, towards the most famous sea in history.

As my car gently slalomed down the slope, I could see from my vantage point why the Israelis call the Sea of Galilee *Kinneret*. It truly is shaped like a *harp*. About thirteen miles in length by eight miles across, it is jewel-like in its beauty. On its western shore lies Tiberias, at this moment starkly white in the last light of the day. I could imagine the old rabbis of history, dusty from walking the Tiberias streets, clustered in their *yeshivas*, patiently dissecting the Law, faithfully creating over a four-hundred-year span the precious Talmud, Judaism's brilliant interpretation of Moses' commands.

Suddenly my reverie was interrupted by a switchback and a side road on my left—the entry to the Mount of Beatitudes. I braked and turned in, as I always did. I could never pass the place where the most famous sermon of all time was preached. I had, and have, a homing instinct to the Sermon on the Mount. Every time I get there, whether to the text or to the physical location, it's like I've returned to the place where I was born.

Pictures of the Mount of Beatitudes don't do it justice. Neither, interestingly, does the real-world view of it from Tiberias. Indeed, as you travel the road around the lake, looking to its northern end, the mount above doesn't look mountain-like at all. It appears to be a mere hill, a minor slope, about two-thirds of the way up to the Upper Galilee on the horizon. But, when you stand on its summit, looking down at the lake hundreds of feet below, you have a great sense of height with a breathtaking vista. It's as though you're standing on the edge of the earth, gazing on another world.

You look down, and there is Capernaum, nestled on the shore of the lake. Just a short distance to the right, also on the shore, is Tabgha. Out on the lake, fishing boats, a few tour boats, and—gasp!—a windsurfer! (You can be sure not a few of the pilgrims on the tour boats have already opined on the sacrilege of utilizing the *sacred* waters for recreation.) Straight ahead, a misty shore, fuzzily outlined with *kibbutzim*. And, even though you can't see it, you know the Jordan River starts there in that haze, beginning its descent (the "Downrusher") to the Dead Sea, about 1,500 feet below sea level.

I pull into the parking area, finding a shady spot beneath a large eucalyptus tree. The Upper Galilee is rife with eucalyptus, imported from Australia in the early 1900s to help the *kibbutzniks* drain the malarial Hula Valley. They've done their work (the Hula is now covered with verdant fields) and are seen by modern Israelis as large, hulking weeds. But, they throw great shade—and, in Israel, you're always looking for shade. Next to my car is a small refreshment kiosk operated by an amiable Christian Arab. He specializes in fresh-squeezed orange juice. I go over, exchange pleasantries, and order a glass. As he squeezes the juice from plump oranges I look around at the familiar scene.

To my left is a stately residential building housing Roman Catholic nuns. It is surrounded by beautiful gardens leading to a uniquely shaped chapel constructed of basalt stone and Italian marble. Built with funds supplied by Mussolini toward the end of the Second World War, it stands on the edge of the downslope to the Sea of Galilee, commanding an awesome view. Dignified and minimalist, it is visited by thousands of pilgrims every year. Right now, as I look at it, there's not a tourist to be seen. The Arab hands me the juice. I take slow sips, looking straight ahead, down to the Sea, and I see my favorite spot inviting me over.

Twelve large boulders form a rough circle beneath three tall trees. The circle is about twenty feet in diameter and is on a tilt with the slope. Each boulder is large enough to perch on or lean against. As I sit at the base of the uppermost stone, I imagine this as the place where Jesus sat down to teach his disciples, each leaning or sitting in his turn on or against the other rocks. Perhaps this is the spot where the greatest sermon in history was given. I reach for the small New Testament in my pants pocket. I turn to the opening verses of Matt 5. The words come alive: "One day as he saw the crowds gathering, Jesus went up on the mountainside and sat down. His disciples gathered around him, and he began to teach them."

Seems Jesus was crowd-averse at times. Here he escapes the teeming masses at the lakeshore and climbs to the top of the hill with his disciples. He sits down (rabbis sat to teach), his disciples join him, and the teaching begins.

## Blessed Are the Poor in Spirit, for Theirs Is the Kingdom of Heaven

There's an old saying that "big doors swing on small hinges." I don't think it an overstatement to say the entire Sermon on the Mount hinges on Jesus' opening words. Indeed, one could say that the sole entry-level condition for citizenship in the kingdom of heaven is poverty of spirit. Why? Because the polar opposite of spiritual poverty is spiritual pride. And pride, as C. S. Lewis famously put it, is "The Great Sin."[1] It is the ultimate barrier between us and heaven.

There are several Hebrew words in the Old Testament that are translated, in one way or another, as *self-exaltation* or *self-elevation*, or *arrogance*, *loftiness*, *presumption*, or *boastful*. What is made clear is that self-glorification is a fast track to rejection by the Almighty. Human pride is toxic. Heaven spits it out.

Jesus, no doubt, was familiar with the Old Testament's abhorrence of pride. Perhaps as a young student he had read (for example) Isa 2, where the Lord castigates the "descendants of Jacob," who are awash in arrogance:

> 7. [Israel] is full of silver and gold; there is no end to its treasures. Their land is full of warhorses; there is no end to its chariots.
>
> 8. Their land is full of idols; the people worship things they have made with their own hands.
>
> 9. So now they will be humbled, and all will be brought low—do not forgive them.

---

1. A chapter title from Lewis' *Mere Christianity*.

## The Setting

10. Crawl into caves in the rocks. Hide in the dust from the terror of the Lord and the glory of his majesty.
11. Human pride will be brought down, and human arrogance will be humbled. Only the Lord will be exalted on that day of judgment.
12. For the Lord of Heaven's Armies has a day of reckoning. He will punish the proud and mighty and bring down everything that is exalted.
17. Human pride will be humbled, and human arrogance will be brought down. Only the Lord will be exalted on that day of judgment.

As the Old Testament prophet sees it, arrogance results in humiliation. And, in that pride is seen as fueled by material success, abundance must be wiped out: the "silver and gold," the "tall cedars" (Isa 2:7, 13), the "high towers" (Isa 2:15a), the "fortified walls" (Isa 2:15b)—indeed, every material security supporting unrestrained independence is fair game for the devastating "terror of the Lord." Adversity forces mankind to remember its Maker, and exalt him alone. If, as the Old Testament declares, the only security we have is in the Lord, then the truly wealthy are those who place their security in him. What is dross on earth is gold in heaven. Often this world's castoffs are the Lord's princes.

You can be sure the disciples raised an eyebrow or two at these opening words. Even in their time, poverty of any form was looked upon as something evil. The goal was to be self-sufficient. Independence was a virtue. But Jesus was calling his followers to dependence, a message as countercultural in his day as it is in ours. When you get right down to it, no one in history has wanted to be dependent. We want to be independent, our own source and beginning, our own final court of appeal. We don't want to need anyone—especially God. So we pay him lip service and pretty much exclude him from our daily lives. He's the emergency specialist, not "a friend who sticketh closer than a brother" (Prov 18:24 KJV). Jesus' words imply that if you don't need God, he doesn't need you. The kingdom of heaven is all about love for God and one another. The poor in spirit seem to be the only ones who get it. That's why the "kingdom" is "theirs."

Spiritual poverty is not always linked to material lack. We need to remember that it's the "love of money" and not money itself that is the root of evil. Money is morally neutral. And, we all know poor folk who love it a lot. (May we include ourselves here?) As a pastor, I've known many *monied* people who are fully aware of their spiritual poverty and exhibit a humble attitude. Human nature is stronger than material goods; both rich and poor can be humble or swollen with arrogance. But generally, the arrogance of the rich is sustained by lack of want, whereas the arrogance of the poor is sustained by repressed resentment. Maybe this is why the Almighty breaks down "the high tower and every fortified wall" (Isa 2:15), destroys "the great trading ships and every magnificent vessel" (Isa 2:16), and levels "the high mountains and all the lofty hills" (Isa 2:14). He removes the props of the rich and the gall of the poor. He creates a level playing field where all are equally spiritually impoverished. Then he can welcome them into the kingdom of heaven.

So, the general goal is the kingdom of heaven, and the general qualification for entry is spiritual poverty. Now, Jesus goes on to describe what the poor in spirit are like.

## Blessed Are They That Mourn, for They Shall Be Comforted

The spiritually poor mourn their lack of heaven. Grieve their loss of God. Suffer their *dwelling in darkness*. They know intuitively that they're made for a *far country*. There is a deep-seated dissatisfaction in their soul (indeed, their hymn might be the Rolling Stones's classic "I Can't Get No Satisfaction"). But they don't know how to get to where they belong. Their life is characterized by search and frustration. It's an agony.

These hurting ones are "blessed," Jesus says. Why? Because "they shall be comforted." *Shall*. It's definite. Anyone whose arrogance is broken and suffers the dark night of the soul has unwittingly begun a journey that will culminate in entry. The kingdom of heaven awaits. The search and the frustration will end. Comfort will be theirs.

What we often miss as we travel from darkness to light is that the step-by-step journey changes us. At points along the path we may resist change, and as long as we do so, the trip is suspended. But then we acquiesce to the transformative impact of the long road and the journey continues. What we may not realize is that even as the road bends it bends us. We are becoming meek.

### Blessed Are the Meek, for They Will Inherit the Earth

Meekness is not slump-shouldered obsequiousness where we're constantly deferring to others with a groveling, "No, after you . . ." Rather, in the biblical languages it essentially means a *willingness to being shaped* and an *openness to being molded, malleability*. A meek person is someone who admits he does not know everything and that they've got a lot to learn. You can be very self-confident and very meek at the same time. It has nothing to do with self-esteem. It has everything to do with *God-esteem*. Meek people allow for and expect change. Sometimes they may be reluctant to do so, but in the end they embrace transformation. But it's tough to be meek if you don't acknowledge your spiritual poverty. You've got to be hungry and thirsty.

### Blessed Are Those Who Hunger and Thirst for Righteousness, for They Will Be Filled

In the English language, righteousness and justice are translations of the Hebrew words *tzadkah* and *mishpat*. Righteousness and justice can be used interchangeably (some versions translate righteousness as justice in this beatitude), but usually they have different foci: righteousness refers to the fulfillment of the vertical relationship with God; and justice refers to the fulfillment of the horizontal relationship with neighbor. Jesus summed up God's expectations of us when he said to the inquiring lawyer, "You

## The Setting

must love the Lord your God with all your heart, all your soul, all your mind, and all your strength . . . [and] love your neighbor as yourself" (Mark 12:29–31; see also Deut 6:4–5; Matt 22: 37–40; Luke 10:25–28). You might call this "heaven's mission statement" for citizens of the kingdom. The Old Testament prophets certainly would resonate with Jesus' summary: the bedrock of the prophetic ministry in the Old Testament is the call to righteousness and justice, which suggests two things: (i) righteousness and justice are what God expects of us; and (ii) righteousness and justice are the only *substances* that can satisfy the hunger and thirst of the poor in spirit.

Ironically our hunger and thirst are satisfied not by taking in, but by giving out—by loving God and neighbor. Marching to the beat of heaven's drum is active and dynamic: loving God on the upstroke (righteousness) and loving the broken on the downstroke (justice). And, when faced with issues from our neighbor that overwhelm our capacity to be objective, we remember that mercy trumps justice every time.

### Blessed Are the Merciful, for They Will Be Shown Mercy

The poor in spirit are awash in their need for mercy. The arrogant boast "Lord, I thank you that I am not like other men," whereas the spiritually poor don't dare raise their head, let alone their voice, in the presence of the Lord, except to whisper, "God, be merciful to me, a sinner" (Luke 18:9–14). Rather than beat one's chest in boastful pride, the humble beat their chest in contrition. If God is not merciful, all is lost.

But he is merciful. And those who show mercy *obtain* mercy themselves. It's a constant theme in scripture: you show mercy, love, forgiveness, and compassion to your neighbor, because you've been on the receiving end, and you're so grateful. You can do nothing less.

Indeed, those who are unloving to their neighbor demonstrate they know nothing of the love of God. They may be very religious, full of righteous sounds, but they're spiritually dead, shooting blanks. The spiritually poor have one reflex—and one alone: when faced with injustice, offense, injury, slander, lies, or whatever, they show mercy. Their mantra: "There but for the grace of God go I." Gratitude makes them do it. There's no other motive; their hearts are pure.

### Blessed Are the Pure in Heart, for They Shall See God

Jesus was living in, indeed was a part of, a culture obsessed with cleanliness. *Kosher* defined their lives—if you were religious, that is. The book of Leviticus in the Old Testament goes to great lengths to describe what is clean and unclean: *clean* being the absolute prerequisite to approaching God. *Unclean* and God didn't mix. Thus, the *washed* had access to the heavenlies, the *unwashed* to destruction.

But Jesus taught differently. Again, in a powerfully counterculture way he taught and lived the antithesis of pharisaical purity. With regard to kosher food, he said, "Can't you see that the food you put into your body cannot defile you? Food doesn't go into your heart, but only passes through the stomach and then goes into the sewer. . . . It is what comes from inside that defiles you" (Mark 7:18–19 NLT). As for the unwashed, he bathed himself in them: "But when the teachers of religious law who were Pharisees saw him eating with tax collectors and other sinners, they asked his disciples, 'Why does he eat with such scum?' When Jesus heard this, he told them, 'Healthy people don't need a doctor—sick people do. I have come to call not those who think they are righteous, but those who know they are sinners'" (Mark 2:16–17 NLT). He even went so far as to touch and heal lepers, mix socially with gentiles and Samaritans, and, in essence, offend every *purity of the outside* rule and regulation in his Jewish culture. He did this not for the sake of rebellion, but for the sake of an essential truth: purity comes not from the outward show of things, but from the inside, the heart.

This teaching took the breath away. The disciples, as Jews, had a *theology of the outside*, but they were deficient in a *theology of the inside.* They would be flat-footed in any avoidance reflex as Jesus threw this at them. Purity of the heart? What's that?

Perhaps it had something to do with agendas. The pure in heart had no secret agenda, no manipulative methods, no personal aggrandizement in mind as they lived their lives. Their spiritual impoverishment had stripped them of any sense of entitlement, any *rights* to demand, any call for God to vindicate them. Like the tax collector in the temple, their only position was prostration. They were totally in God's hands. It was "thy will be done, not mine." They were empty vessels, ready to be filled with God's glory. And, Jesus says, they will be filled and they will see. Whereas the self-righteous are blind, the spiritually broken are sighted. And their vista is God.

I look up from my Bible. A shepherd has just walked into the picture, grazing his sheep on the slope beneath me. Unaware of my presence he has just picked up a young lamb and is carefully extracting a thorn from its nose. The lamb is bleating wildly, thrashing its legs, and making every effort to escape what must be a painful process. The mother ewe paces about, uttering threats and looking darkly at the shepherd, but he is undeterred. Another brief moment or two and the lamb is free, running quickly to its mother and thrusting its muzzle into her udder. Now he can drink again. Thanks but no thanks to the shepherd. "He hurt me, Mama! He hurt me!" No connection between the *wounding* and the drinking. The shepherd and the lamb inhabit the same space but live in parallel universes.

Rather like us humans, I think. So near to God, and yet so far. Blaming him when things go wrong and hurt us. Making no linkage between our sufferings and our blessings. Thinking it's all about us. And yet . . .

There is this need, this powerful urge, to bridge the gap, to ascend to the throne room, to talk with our Maker. He's created us for this—indeed, it's the *godlike* aspect of our nature. We can talk with him, hear from him, and commune with him. We call it prayer.

## The Setting

I've got to leave. I'm late. I wanted to be in Jerusalem at dusk. My family and I are celebrating *Kabbalat Shabat* (the Welcoming of the Sabbath) tonight with dear friends. But before I leave, I want to pray. I turn a few pages past the Beatitudes, and there, still part of Jesus' Sermon on the Mount, is the ultimate prayer—the prayer Jesus said we should pray. I do so, alone but for the unseen nuns, the kiosk keeper, and the shepherd. As I pray, I open the windows of my soul, and the glories of his light and love flood in.

# The Windows

> I remember, I remember,
> The house where I was born
> The little window where the sun
> Came peeping in at morn.
>
> —Thomas Hood, "I remember," 1826

As I write I'm sitting at a window. It is a familiar place. It has been my thinking place as well as my writing place for several years. But this time it is different. The trees are budding, the birds are building nests, the squirrels endlessly running here and there—but there are no people. The coronavirus has forced everyone indoors. Social isolation is the new norm. Only history will tell us how long this global scourge lasts. It's a scary time. At this point the world seems on the brink of collapse. Yet, it may be on the brink of a new beginning as I suggested in a blog I had posted:

> The ongoing COVID-19 pandemic is an unwelcome adventure, but adventure nonetheless. The *Oxford Dictionary* calls an adventure "a daring enterprise; a hazardous activity," which this crisis certainly is. No doubt it's "hazardous," but there are also many elements of "enterprise." There are several burgeoning medical breakthroughs in potential vaccines, the repurposing of proven antiretrovirals, and societal revisioning involving everything from how and where we work to relearning relational

skills. New horizons are being forced upon us, which may be catalytic to innovations and inventions that otherwise would never have been considered. Then there's the spiritual renewal. Prayers, hymns, and a new softheartedness to faith have emerged, along with a rediscovery of kindness. It would appear to be true that "every cloud has a silver lining . . ."

The ironic thing about windows is that even as they let the light in, they can reveal darkness (both without and within). A window can bless and blame, which is why we sometimes prefer to draw the shades. As the Scriptures say, a common human default is to prefer darkness to light when our behavior is questionable. But, setting the moral philosophy aside, we all prefer a window to a wall. Perhaps the greatest punishment of solitary confinement is the windowless cell.

In a sense windows are three dimensional: there's an outside, an inside, and an observer. A window has little relevance without someone who is looking through the glass. The pane is invisible, yet it can reflect the light even as it protects from rain, wind and cold. It even provides a sense of security. Now, I'm fully aware that analogies break down sooner or later, but let's agree that a window is truly a marvelous thing.

Before we get to the ten windows opened by the Lord's Prayer, a few general observations are in order. First of all, there are two instances in the Gospels where Jesus taught his disciples to pray. Matthew's record (Matt 6:9–13) occurs in the context of the famous Sermon on the Mount (Matt 5–7), and Luke's account (Luke 11:2–4) takes place in an unknown location or in a "certain place" (Luke 11:1) after Jesus had been at prayer. Both teachings are for the disciples' benefit, and he may have taught on the subject more often than on these two occasions in that "men more frequently require to be reminded than informed."[1] Nevertheless, the two prayers are similar in content, although the Matthew

---

1. Samuel Johnson, *The Works of Samuel Johnson, LL.D., in Nine Volumes, Volume the Second: The Rambler, Volume I* (London, 1825; Project Gutenberg, 2013), no. 2, https://www.gutenberg.org/files/43656/43656-h/43656-h.htm.

account contains two more petitions than Luke's. I see no need to jump through hoops trying to explain why the two prayers are not identical.

I say this for two reasons: (i) as a preacher myself I've often preached the same sermon many times, but every time I do, the presentation in terms of emphases and flow is fluid, adapted to the time, place and audience; and (ii) the gospels are not the product of collaboration by committee. Each record stands on its own.

Then, of course, there's context. It's the immediate setting that is intriguing. Matthew recounts Jesus' words before the Prayer, where he makes it clear that prayer is not a show (Matt 6:5), is private (Matt 6:6), should be brief (Matt 6:7), and is always productive (Matt 6:8) in that God, not us, knows what the real need is and factors that into his response ("no" is just as much an answer to prayer as is "yes," with "wait" always in the wings). After the Prayer, Jesus reminds the disciples that forgiveness of others must be present in our prayer posture (Matt 6:14–15). Humility, grace, and gratitude (all underlying a forgiving attitude) are vital components in our integrity as believers. Unforgiveness compromises all prayer.

In Luke, the teaching on prayer is a brief response to just one of the disciples who, apparently moved by seeing Jesus at prayer, asked for some coaching. Without preamble, Jesus taught much the same prayer as that in Matthew, but he concludes the teaching with an affirmation of "audacity" (from the Greek *importunity, shamelessness*) in prayer with three action steps: "Ask—Seek—Knock" (Luke 11:8–13). The ultimate gift from the Father is "the Holy Spirit" (Luke 11:13c).

So, even though the Lord's Prayer[2] has been the liturgical prayer of the church over centuries, it is more a guide than a formula. But what a guide! As we're about to see, praying the Lord's Prayer opens the windows of our souls.

2. Author's Note: Some, but not all, of extant manuscripts of Matthew include the doxology "for thine is the kingdom, the power and the glory, for ever and ever. Amen." Most Protestants conclude the prayer this way, and Roman Catholics do not. It is not a point of contention. Rather it reflects tradition and history. All agree that the "glory" is the Lord's.

Window No. 1: Identity

"Our Father" tells us something powerful about who we are. We are God's children. But, more powerful still, it tells us who God is. He is Father of all. In this chapter, we look at a summary of some of God's attributes as well as both who he is as Creator and who we are as his creation. And we'll discuss what Genesis means when we read, "So God created mankind in his own image" (Gen 1:27). So, this chapter is foundational to all succeeding chapters.

Window No. 2: Family

"Our" means *us*. In biblical terms, we are the "sons of God" (meaning *daughters* as well), the *people of God*, and the *family of God*. In this chapter the focus will be on the extended family or clan that predominated in Hebrew history. In the course of this examination, we look at some of the implications of that little word *our*.

Window No. 3: Home

It's quite a stretch when we pray "in heaven." We lightly say "heaven is my home," but what does that mean? And what are we thinking of, or visualizing, when we speak of God as sitting on his throne in heaven? Then there's the apostle Paul talking about a "third heaven"! (2 Cor 12:2). What's up with that? This is a huge subject and I'll only be able to scratch the surface.

Window No. 4: Worship

"Hallowed" means *holy*. Before God is anything, he is holy. As an adjective modifying the noun *name* it is very powerful, in that "the Name" in Scripture is equivalent to "God." So to invoke "the Holy Name" is to invite the very presence of the Almighty into your life. In this chapter, we tackle these two big words. *Holy* and *Name* capture the very essence of the divine.

Window No. 5: Humility

The singular focus of worship is "thy" name. Worship is not about us, but about our Maker. It's God's glory, not ours, that is celebrated. This, of course, means that we as worshipers must have perspective: "God is in heaven and you are on earth, so let your words be few" (Eccl 5:2). *Ascribe worth* (worship) to God from a posture of humility. Spiritual pride won't cut it.

Window No. 6: Accountability

We all know what a kingdom is, but very few of us have lived in one. Countries which are still part of the British Commonwealth have a titular monarch, but are not subject to governing oversight from Buckingham Palace. There are a few very small kingdoms in the world where subjects are subject to a ruler, but in general the days of kings and queens are over, so there is a disconnect when we pray "thy kingdom come." But, the very first message Jesus preached was "repent, for the kingdom of heaven has come near" (Matt 4:17). In this chapter, we look at the vital subject of the kingdom of God. For Jesus' disciples, it had both immediate and future implications especially with regard to accountability.

Window No. 7: Purpose

The Lord's Prayer may be the perfect pattern for prayer, but the pivotal prayer is that which Jesus prayed in the Garden of Gethsemane just before his arrest and crucifixion: "Not my will, but thine be done" (Matt 26:39 KJV). To freely submit our will to the will of God is a lifelong challenge. We continually resist. In this chapter, we look at the will of God in general as it's described in the Bible and we'll discuss the often thorny issue of God's will as it relates to our daily lives and values.

Window No. 8: Simplicity

In our Western world, a prayer for "daily bread" seems to lack relevance. Affluence has raised the bar in terms of our needs. Even though there are many who rely on soup kitchens and food banks our culture tends to marginalize and rationalize the poverty of our urban centers. We prefer our ever-expanding entitlements. In this chapter, we see how the Lord's Prayer refocuses our values and reminds us of our vulnerabilities and dependence on the providence of God. Our only *entitlement* is his grace.

Window No. 9: Forgiveness

Jesus made it very clear that there was a distinct tie between God's forgiveness of our sins against him and our forgiveness of the sins of others against us. It's a moral no-brainer: if we refuse to forgive others, how can we with any integrity expect God to forgive us? Forgiveness is utterly crucial to salvation.

Window No. 10: Courage

Usually, when we think about temptation, we think about morality. We certainly are aware of the beguilement of money, power, and status, but sex seems to dominate most temptation scenarios. Nevertheless, we'll see in this chapter that Jesus was referring to a deeper temptation—the possibility of giving in to religious persecution (that is, denying one's faith in God when under pressure from religious/governmental authorities where *the rack* threatens life and limb). Then, the motivator of this evil is none other than "the evil one"—Satan himself. This is why Jesus teaches us to pray that the Lord will protect us from both apostasy under persecution as well as the very one who seeks "to kill and destroy." We're to trust God and take courage.

# Window No. 1
# Identity

> Her conception of God was certainly not orthodox. She felt towards Him as she might have felt towards a glorified sanitary engineer; and in some of her speculations she seems hardly to distinguish between the Deity and the Drains.
>
> —*Eminent Victorians*, 1918: "Florence Nightingale"

To address God as "Our Father" was not unusual in Jesus' day. "Abinu, Malkenu" ("Our Father, our King") was heard every day in the synagogues. This concept of God as Father was rooted in the Hebrew Scriptures: "Isn't he your Father who created you?" (Deut 32:6 NLT); "Are we not all children of the same Father?" (Mal 2:10 NLT); "Surely you are still our Father!" (Isa 63:16 NLT); "And yet, O Lord, you are our Father" (Isa 64:8 NLT); "Father you have been my guide since my youth" (Jer 3:4 NLT); "I would love to treat you as my own children" (Jer 3:19 NLT).

Even though most of Israel's interaction with God was temple-centric, formal, and liturgical, there were definite relational components. "Deep" was free to call unto deep (Ps 42:7). The lines of communication were always open between *I* and *Thou*.

There are literally thousands of books and essays in the libraries of the world and online that discuss the nature of God. Many of them can be quite daunting. Theology requires a certain philosophical predisposition on the part of both writer and reader. A low-key, casual approach seems to be a nonstarter, if not disrespectful. I took that "road less traveled" when I was pastoring in Jerusalem and wrote *Theology for Non-Theologians*, which was published by Macmillan. My challenge as I write is to resist the temptation to write another book on theology. I'm going to try to limit my thoughts to what the Lord's Prayer tells us about God in the broader context of the windows it opens.

As you will experience as we journey through the Prayer window by window, the greater theme of God's attributes, or personality, shines throughout. To refer to God as Father means among other things that he is a person. He is not named as the God of trees, rocks, and hills (although these "sing his praises"), but he is called "the God of Abraham, Isaac, and Jacob." He is a personal God who relates to persons: he speaks to Adam (Gen 3:8–9), covenants with Abraham (Gen 12:1–3), and talks with Moses (Exod 3), person to person.

Yet, even as he loves us, knows our names, and supplies our earthly needs "according to his riches," those "riches" are "in glory" (Phil 4:19)—in other words, *in heaven*. God is Spirit.

The second verse of the Bible says, "The earth was formless and empty, and darkness covered the deep waters. And the Spirit of God was hovering over the surface of the waters" (Gen 1:2 NLT). Jesus said, "God is Spirit, and his worshipers must worship in spirit and in truth" (John 4:24). In Hebrew, *spirit* conveys *air in motion*. In other words *spirit* means life. This indicates that our living, loving Father can think (intellect), feel (emotion), and choose (will). He is fully self-aware and self-determined. Indeed, he is all-powerfully so. When he introduced himself to Moses (Exod 3:14), he identified himself as "I Am" (YHWH—Hebrew: "I will be what/who I will be"). Only one can make such a statement of self-determination. The Eternal Creator and Father of all that is is that one. His attributes (such as eternality, perfection, omniscience, omnipresence, etc.) are unique to him. But the bottom line is his holiness.

"Hallowed be thy name" captures it. Before God is anything, he is holy. Holiness is at the very core of his being, which means he is morally perfect and pure. Ultimately, it means he is forever distinct from his creation. Pantheism, which characterizes a few religious systems (including animism), declares that God is the universe and the universe is God. Not so, says the Bible. The universe is distinctly separate from God. It is flawed, gradually declining, and in a few more billions of years will undergo its *heat death* and forever pass away. God, however, is forever apart from his creation. He does sustain it by his word, but he will never pass away. He is "the same yesterday, today, and forever" (Heb 13:8). Indeed, his holiness in the final analysis is his *apartness*.

"Thy kingdom come" speaks of his self-awareness and purpose. It is *his* kingdom, comprising much more than the church. It is the entirety of creation, past, present, and future, bearing *his* signature. Only he knows the plan; only he can execute it. That's why we submit to his Lordship and his purpose. Any *advice* we give him in those all-too-often self-centered prayers are nothing but a conceit: "God is in heaven and you are on earth; therefore let your words be few" (Eccl 5:2b). Then, when we pray "thy will be done," we're not only acceding to his sovereignty, but we're acknowledging that there really is only one will in the universe—and it is his.

It is his love and grace alone that allow us even to speak. This is *his* world, not ours. We're mere tenants. But, he *does* enjoy our company. His question to Adam in the garden of Eden, "Where are you?" (Gen 3:9) echoes down through history. Our Father seeks us out. He wants to talk. And if we'll let him, he'll make tenants into his very own children. Indeed, "the Lord knows those that are his" (2 Tim 2:19).

So, what does it mean when Genesis says, "Let us make mankind in our image, in our likeness, so that they may rule over the fish in the sea and the birds in the sky, over the livestock and all the wild animals, and over all the creatures that move along the ground" (Gen 1:26)? I'll leave the plural pronouns, the singular verbs and the plural word for God—"Elohim" (the singular is "El")—for the theologians to explain. It's the words "image" and "likeness" that interest me. Adam was made in God's "image" and "likeness." This is explained in the sentence as God giving Adam dominion as vice-regent over God's creation. King David poetically describes humankind as super-stewards (Ps 8):

> 3. When I consider your heavens, the work of your fingers, the moon and the stars, which you have set in place,
> 4. What is mankind that you are mindful of them, human beings that you care for them?
> 5. You have made them a little lower than the angels, and crowned them with glory and honor.
> 6. You made them rulers over the works of your hands; you put everything under their feet:
> 7. All flocks and herds, and the animals of the wild,
> 8. The birds in the sky, and the fish in the sea, all that swim the paths of the seas.

The image is not physical, but spiritual, intellectual, and moral. Mankind rules over God's creation with executive authority. And we're able to do so with intellect, emotion, and will. Flora, fauna, and environment are ours to steward. This is our Father's world, and we are its guardians.

# Identity

## Homer

I come from a family of prairie preachers. My great-grandfather Peter and his four sons were both farmers and church planters. They were a hardworking, ebullient family, entrepreneurial, good-humored, and betrayed their Irish immigrant roots with *the gift of the gab*. They loved to tell stories. They were also known as *strongmen*, my grandfather Howard the strongest of them all.

Grandpa dropped out of school in grade three. This was not uncommon in those days. Farmers relied on family for labor, thus the stereotypical large number of children (eight to twelve kids was ideal!). Book learning was not a value but working the soil was. As soon as children were able the chores were assigned. Working from dawn to dusk was matter of course. You worked hard, you ate hardy, and you slept well.

Grandpa's strength became evident early on. Even as a toddler he used to love lifting things. It seemed anything stationary was a target—chairs, rocks, wagons, even the occasional barnyard goat! (The goat would always butt him away, but as he rose from the dirt there was a look on Grandpa's little face that said, "Just you wait!") As he grew into his teen years, he was often seen lifting farm equipment, one end of the harrow, a rear tractor wheel, an abandoned rusty plough; but his favorite lift involved squats with an iron anvil cradled in his arms.

All strong men meet their match sooner or later. One day in his early twenties, Grandpa was sitting on the heavy wooden fence surrounding the cattle pen. A young bull calf, frisky and lacking wisdom (he was only a few months old), saw Grandpa perched there and decided to knock him off. Head down and snorting he charged. The fence, made of telephone poles, shook with the blow but held. Undeterred the young bull charged again. Even though Grandpa wasn't touched, he declared to one of his brothers who was watching, "This young fella needs a lesson. I'm gonna fix him!" (A favorite expression of his when he was about to put someone in their place.) So he leaped down into the pen and challenged the adolescent bovine to bring it on. His plan was to sidestep the charge, lift Mickey (the bull's name) and throw him to the ground. It hadn't occurred to him that Mickey already weighed four hundred pounds. Mickey charged, Grandpa slipped, and it was a train wreck. In the Old English fashion, Grandpa "measured his length upon the ground," Mickey sauntered away in triumph, and it took three days for the concussion to abate. The story, related countlessly through the years at family gatherings, always produced volumes of loud, unbridled hooting and snorting laughter.

Grandpa's second son, Homer, also had the gift of strength. He never resorted to strapping one end of a rope across his chest and tying the other end to a car's bumper and then pulling (!) it out of a muddy ditch (as Grandpa did), but he did a lot of lifting. For him, lifting was like a vocation. When he saw something heavy he was compelled to test his strength. One Sunday morning in his early teens, he eyed a Model A Ford parked outside the Odd Fellows Hall in town. Grandpa was holding services there because like most prairie church planters he could not afford a purpose-built building. The car belonged to *the wealthiest* congregant. Most of the people came to church by horse-drawn wagon. One or two farmers drove tractors to the service, while a few came on foot. Homer, who had been climbing a tree (another of his compulsions), arrived late to the service. The Ford beckoned. Seeing that no one was watching, he bent to the task. Gripping the front bumper he straightened up, lifting the front end to the point where the front wheels were almost off the ground. Suddenly there was a loud snap and the bumper came off. He stood there embarrassed and amazed. He left the bumper on the ground and meekly walked into church. Grandpa was mortified and much more than the Model A's owner. He told Homer he would have to work the debt off in free labor at the man's farm. The farmer was pleased. He knew Homer was as good as two men. And he was.

Homer was my father. He and my mother were married upon his return from infantry duty in Europe during the Second World War. Mom was eighteen years old and dad twenty-three on their wedding day. I was born eleven months later. They took me to their humble home after a life-threatening (for Mom) delivery. It was a lean-to attached to a small church building out in a farmer's field surrounded by prairies and an unobstructed 360-degree horizon. Heat in this uninsulated shed was supplied by a small potbellied woodstove. In the sometimes minus-forty-degree winter temperatures, Mom would put me to bed in a snowsuit to sleep at night.

Dad's strength probably saved my life that first winter. When I was three months old, a ten-day prairie blizzard swept central Alberta. The roads were blocked with drifts of whirling snow. The temperatures hovered in the minus-twenty-to-thirty-degree range. Everything stopped. The lives of the elderly and the very young were at risk as people sheltered in their isolated farm houses. Some of them ran out of wood for their wood stoves and began burning furniture. Mom ran out of milk.

At that time breastfeeding was out of fashion, so Mom bottle-fed me with canned Carnation milk. In the middle of the storm there were only two cans left. Dad knew what he had to do. He set out in the blizzard to walk five miles across the fields to a country store. The snow was thigh-high, sometimes waist-high. Keeping the telephone poles bordering the county road in sight he braced himself against the wind and fought his way to Pat's General Store. Pat and his family lived next door and were surprised to hear someone knocking. They quickly opened the store and sold "the reverend" a case of forty-eight cans of Carnation. Lifting the heavy box to his shoulder, he began the slog home with Pat's warning that it was too dangerous and he should wait out the storm at their place. Dad, of course, wouldn't hear of it. His nineteen-year-old wife and three-month-old son needed him *and* the milk. He followed the furrow he had ploughed through the snow that in places was already drifted over. At one point, in exhaustion, he dropped the box to take a breather and thought maybe he should lie down for a bit. In the mental fog of hypothermia, this seemed a good idea. But, like a jolt of electricity originating somewhere in the depths of his brain, he realized that lying down would mean death. He picked up the box and by sheer strength of will made it home. My anxious mother thanked God and I had my bottle, oblivious to Dad's heroic feat.

There are many stories I could tell of Dad's amazing strength. He pastored small churches in small towns and was always the strongest man. Kids loved him. They used to line up as he threw them way over his head (he was six foot three) and caught them as they screamed with delight. He was always first choice when the farmers needed extra labor during harvesting. They respected and loved him. And he loved them. He loved God, Mom, his kids, and his congregation—in that order. He was a gentle giant and to my everlasting joy and security, he was my dad and I was his son.

As I grew older I met many kids in the neighborhood and at school who didn't have what I had. Their fathers were abusive, or alcoholic, unfaithful, and sometimes absent. They suffered from a father-gap. Their lives were not whole. Maybe this was why they were drawn to my dad. Decades later, he was still a magnet. He eventually pastored hundreds of young pastors. They couldn't get enough of him. He was a *mentor* long before *mentoring* became a word in our cultural glossary. And did I say it already? He was my father!

So it's no surprise that when I learned the Lord's Prayer I had no trouble at all calling God "Our Father." I had been bathed in my earthly father's gentle strength and love and the word "Father" was a no-brainer. All my life I have felt secure and loved. My Dad and my heavenly Father have given me a sure foundation. My identity is unassailable because "Our Father" is my protector, and he *loves* me! How good is that?

*Identity*

# Window No. 1
# Prayer

Forever Father

O matchless, merciful
Holy One!
Our hearts are stilled
In your presence.
To think that we are
Yours . . .
You the one who made
All that is—
The heavens, moon and stars
A universe eternally vast,
Yet this tiny jewel on which
We live
Is home to your ultimate genius
In creating us godlike creatures
Who like you think, feel, and act.
Tis too much to grasp.
Yet we believe.
Our hearts swell with
The longing for home.
Home where you are,
Forever Father.
We are forever yours.

## Window No. 2
# Family

> We, your blood family, will do all we can to continue the imaginative way in which you were steering these two exceptional young men so that their souls are not simply immersed by duty and tradition but can sing openly as you planned.
>
> —LORD SPENCER, IN HIS FUNERAL TRIBUTE TO DIANA, PRINCESS OF WALES, SEP 7, 1997

In biblical days marriage was patriarchal and the family large. Father, mother (mothers—polygamy was common), concubines, children, servants, slaves (with their children), grandparents, and assorted other relatives made for a clan if not a small town. Everyone had a distinct and strict family identity with the name and rule of the father sacrosanct. The family was both an economic unit and a religious community, its integrity and sustainability maintained by a moral code adjudicated by the clan leaders (fathers and/or elders). Adultery, for instance, was severely punished (usually by stoning) because it was a direct assault on the integrity of the family as well as a *theft* of property. In Israelite culture, no man was an island.

At the very beginning God commanded that mankind should "Be fruitful and increase in number" (Gen 1:28). Children were vital to the biblical family. Sons were the priority; in 2 Kgs 10:1 we are told that King Ahab of Israel had seventy of them. Daughters, of course, were of great value in terms of mothering sons and in the forging of alliances between clans and nations via marriage (more about sons and daughters later). Suffice to say that biblical families abounded in children.

In the Hebrew there are two words for children: *banim* (sons) and *yeledim* (children) can be used interchangeably, but *banim* is usually employed. *Children* is generic and inclusive; it refers to both sexes, and sometimes is used to denote the nation (e.g., the children of Israel). As a nation, the children of Israel were a covenant community. God had initiated it and it was to be remembered and honored as we are told in Isa 59:21: "As for me, this is my covenant with them, says the Lord. My Spirit who is on you, will not depart from you, and my words that I have put in your mouth will always be on your lips, on the lips of your children and on the lips of their descendants from this time on and forever."

And in Isa 29:23: "When they see among them their children, the work of my hands, they will keep my name holy; they will acknowledge the holiness of the Holy One of Jacob, and will stand in awe of the God of Israel."

So, in a very real sense the children of Israel were also the children of the covenant. As such they were part of something much bigger than themselves, something that transcended the nation and the passage of time (Ps 105 NLT):

> 7. He is the Lord our God. His justice is seen throughout the land.
> 8. He always stands by his covenant, the commitment he made to a thousand generations.
> 9. This is the covenant he made with Abraham and the oath he swore to Isaac.
> 10. He confirmed it to Jacob as a decree, and to the people of Israel as a never-ending covenant.

The Israelites may have thought that God was theirs, when in fact they were *his*. God had initiated the covenant with

Abraham and that promise had been to "all the families of the earth" (Gen 12:3c). All men and women of faith throughout the centuries would comprise "the family of God." This is why the possessive pronoun when we pray is "our" and not "my."

When Jesus taught his disciples to pray, he was addressing many more than *the Twelve*. Even though this dozen were the inner circle of Jesus' followers, it is clear there was an even more intimate grouping, an inner core known as *the Three* (Peter, James, John). Then there were *the Seventy-Two* (Luke 10:1–2), who were part of the original company of evangelists commissioned by Jesus to work the "Lord's harvest." All of these persons were men, but there was yet a larger group that accompanied Jesus, and in this larger group were many women. Jesus had a high view of his female followers. The family of God could not exist without mothers and daughters.

There is no doubt that house-churches adjunct to weekly synagogue attendance (early Christians were Jews) became the norm for the early church. Luke summarizes the first days of Christian community in Acts 2:42: "They devoted themselves to the apostles' teaching and to fellowship, to the breaking of bread and to prayer." These hymn-singing, Scripture-reading, praying believers outgrew the physical precincts of the synagogue with its weekly rhythms and protocols. They met on a daily basis, and they met as families. It was no surprise that they saw themselves as the family of God or that they referred to each other as *brother* or *sister*. Theirs was a family faith, and the *Father* was *ours*.

This is why corporate prayer—"*Our* Father"—is just as much a part of the equation as solitary prayer. Even when praying alone we all tend to *Our* rather than *My* Father. Most of our lives are spent in an active or passive communal context. Solitude is not really solitude; our food, clothing, shelter, and safety all depend on the work of others. The grocer, tailor, builder, and first responders all play a role even as we may choose to self-isolate. Yes, I can rightly (hopefully humbly) say *he is My God*, but the fact is he is *Our God*. There is no father if there is no family.

## Living Waters

Dad was ordained with a denomination that reached from coast-to-coast in Canada. Most of their churches were small with congregations comprised of less than fifty souls per church. Some of the smallest of the small were dotted throughout the rural regions of Manitoba, Saskatchewan, and Alberta. Each province had a summer camp for *revival meetings*.

Saskatchewan's camp was located a few miles outside the town of Watrous. It was called "Living Waters," which was a bit of a misnomer in that it had been an abandoned health resort, in sore need of renovation, built on a small lake with a specific density greater than that of the Dead Sea in Israel. Lake Manitou was, as the farmers used to say, "deader'n a doornail!" It was so salty and buoyant that an uninitiated bathing enthusiast almost popped back out of the hole in the water he made when diving in. He would quickly retreat, his eyes and nose burning, his mouth gasping and his skin turning white with salt crystals in the intense summer sun. Those who knew better would ease into the water and float, the upper half of their reclining bodies high and dry. One veteran used to read his bible as he bobbed like a cork in the gentle waves, casting smug glances at the rookies calling loudly for fresh water to rinse their ravaged eyes and nostrils (and any cut or skin lesion would also cry for mercy in the brackish assault). "Living Waters" was anything but living. It was a statement of faith!

During the two weeks of camp meeting the adults spent their midmornings in the *tabernacle*, an old wooden structure with roughly cut rectangles for ventilation (no windows or screens), wooden shingles that passed for a roof, rough-hewn planks for benches, and wood shavings on the floor, presumably to keep the dust down. This was the *adult Bible study*. While this was happening—with a lot of singing, praying, and preaching over the course of two hours or so—the children gathered in the *children's tabernacle*, an abandoned granary. We sat on the backless wooden benches as the *children's evangelist* presented a kid-sized version of the gospel with lots of action songs and flannel-graph depictions of the stories of Jesus. It was fun.

I was five years old the summer that Miss Brown was the children's evangelist. Over the course of two weeks she took us through a child-sized version of John Bunyan's *Pilgrim's Progress* (second only to the Bible as the all-time bestseller). She was more than an anomaly in our religious subculture in that she was attending university studying for a master's degree in English literature. Some of the more fundamentalist pastors opined that she had chosen *head knowledge* over *heart knowledge*. As for me, I thought she was terrific.

One morning as she taught I felt a presence I had never felt before. I was rooted to my seat. She closed in prayer, the other children burst out into the sunshine to play, but I couldn't move. My eyes were welling with tears. Miss Brown came over to me, asking if I was okay. From my very depths I blurted, "Miss Brown I need to get saved!"

Five-year-old boys don't have much residual guilt. There's no sordid past, no drug abuse, no law breaking, no sexual history . . . innocence prevails. Yet I was overcome by an urgent need for a savior. How? It wasn't hypnotism (if it were, I was the only one of thirty children to succumb to the auto-suggestion) nor was it behavior therapy. I was very happy at home, awash in the love of my parents. I don't recall even having an evil thought. No. This was something else (or should I say "someone else"?). Miss Brown kindly led me to a small back room, took my hands and prayed for me. Then she asked me to pray. I wept as I tried to express what was in my heart to God. My eyes flowed, my nose ran, and my confession was more sobs than words. But it wasn't for sorrow, it was for joy. I felt as though a bucket of warm oil had been poured on my head, flowing to my feet. And the room seemed bathed in light. I, of course, had no critical, intellectual skills to rationalize or interpret. It was all experience—a boy meeting his Maker.

Miss Brown thoughtfully left me, suggesting I come outside when I was ready (she knew I'd be embarrassed if seen by my friends with swollen eyes and a runny nose). I stayed a minute or so, checked for onlookers, and quickly ran to the back outside wall of the granary and sat, leaning against the warm siding, my head overshadowed by the long prairie grass. I sat for an hour, my soul awash in total peace. It was my first and most powerful encounter ever with "peace that passeth understanding."

Not yet wanting to run into any of my friends, I cautiously peeked around the granary to the open square in the middle of the camp. To my relief there were a few adults, but no kids. As I walked across the square, I suddenly heard, "Jimmy! Jimmy! Come here!"

I looked and it was Bill Cornelius, the young pastor from Canwood who oversaw the overseas missionary work of the district. "Yes, Mr. Cornelius?"

"Jimmy, this Sunday afternoon we're having our missions meeting at the tabernacle. I'm expecting five hundred people. I'd like you to get your dad to write you a five-minute sermon on why we should 'go into all the world to preach the gospel.' You memorize it. Then, in the meeting, I'll call on you to preach it. Will you do that?"

"Sure, Mr. Cornelius. I'll do it."

That Sunday afternoon I preached my first sermon. In a matter of a couple of hours I'd been *saved* and called to preach. My life's course had been set.

It struck me as I preached that first sermon that the people were not only tickled by this boy preacher, but they were proud of him. He was theirs, one of them. It was my first realization of the support and love of a community. The God I had just met in the granary was their God in the tabernacle. He wasn't just my God—he was *our* God. Indeed, he was "Our Father." We all loved him because he first loved us.

## Window No. 2
## Prayer/

### We Are Family

O Lord of all
Fathers, mothers, daughters
And sons,
We exalt you
And praise you for putting
The lonely in families.
Even the orphan
Finds mercy in you,
You O Rock,
Sheltering us beneath your wings.
Gathered as a hen gathers
Her chicks, we are
Protected by your strong arm
Buffered by the fellowship,
Faith, and prayers of our loved ones.
There is joy in our family for
You, our Father, are our peace.
Together we lift up
Your Holy Name. What a blessing to know
Your family
Is ours.

## Window No. 3
# Home

> When I tread the verge of Jordan,
> Bid my anxious fears subside...
>
> —*Praying for Strength*, Peter Williams, 1771

In Israel today there is a term, *meyode primitivi* (very primitive), which is used in a number of ways. When my family and I first moved to Jerusalem, we considered buying some used furniture for our flat in Rehavia. I mentioned this to one of our neighbors who responded, "No. No. You must to buy *hadash* [new]; you don't want *meyode primitivi* [old]." Sometimes it means "antique," and at other times "ancient." It can mean "uneducated" or "out-of-date" too. Regardless, anything *meyode primitivi* is out-of-sync with the times.

One might describe the view of the people of Jesus' day as *meyode primitivi* when it came to the subject of heaven. The earth was flat and exactly where heaven was (and where gods called home) was a mystery (not much has changed). At best it was a feel-good idea without much specificity. Mind you, there were common similes (some borrowed from the neighbors) used:

1. Heaven as a Metal Strip

   Job describes "the skies" as "a cast metal mirror" (Job 37:18). The Hebrew word is *rakia* which literally means "an expansion of broad plates beaten out." This "expanse of heaven" is usually translated as "firmament." Opposite is a rough sketch of how many Hebrews saw the universe; it's a kind of ancient-domed football stadium.

   As you can see in the sketch, the firmament was that horizontal "strip" above the sun, moon, and stars holding back the waters above, allowing wind, snow, and rain to blow and fall through the *doors*, or *windows*, in strategic locations: "He commanded the skies above and opened the doors of the heavens" and "rained down manna for the people to eat" (Ps 78:23–24). When Moses and the seventy elders of Israel looked up from the summit of Mt. Sinai, they "saw" the Lord standing on "something like a pavement made of lapis lazuli as bright blue as the sky" (Exod 24:9–10). This was a vision of the pavement of the heavens.

2. Heaven as a Tent

   There were other similes employed. For instance, the psalmist says, "The Lord wraps himself in light as with a garment; he stretches out the heavens as a tent" (Ps 104:2). Isaiah says much the same: "He sits enthroned above the circle of the earth, and its people are like grasshoppers. He stretches out the heavens like a canopy, and spreads them out like a tent to live in" (Isa 40:22). In the ancient Hebrew view, the world and the people in it were shrouded by a firmament that looked like a garment, tent, or canopy that protected them from the waters above. This would have been the cosmological concept shared by many of the people of Jesus' day. For sure, in their mind, Jesus was speaking truth when he located the Father "in heaven." He was somewhere up there above the firmament. The heavens were his home.

# Home

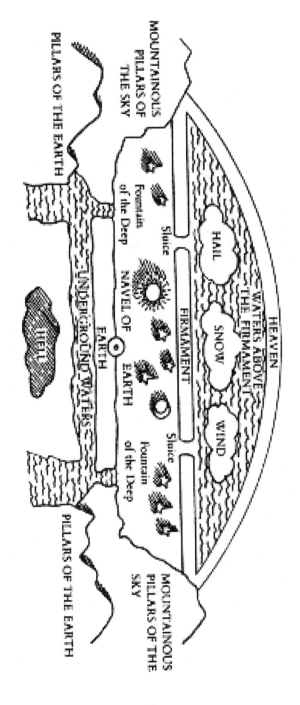

Jesus' audience would have heard of the rabbinic view that there was more than one heaven. The heavens (plural) were composed of at least three: the region of the clouds, the region of the stars, and the vast regions beyond the firmament. Some rabbis even said there were seven. So, a few years after Jesus' resurrection his followers would not have been off-put by the apostle Paul's reference to a third heaven (2 Cor 12:1–4). This vision obviously had a huge impact on Paul as had his conversion on the road to Damascus. Those two visions—one of Christ himself and the other of "paradise" described in verse 4—were enough to energize and sustain him in his arduous missionary journeys, floggings, and stoning. For him heaven was no celestial retirement home.

On the occasion of dedicating the temple, King Solomon implored the Lord to "hear from heaven, your dwelling place" (1 Kgs 8:43). Ezra records the prayer of the Persian king, Cyrus, where he refers to "the Lord the God of heaven" (Ezra 1:2). Moses reminded the Israelites that "the Lord is God in heaven above" (Deut 4:39), and Joshua, Moses' successor, said much the same, "the Lord your God is God in heaven above" (Josh 2:11). These and many other biblical statements made it clear that in the haze and tangle of *meyode primitivi* thoughts and speculations about heaven, the Israelites were united on a singular truth: the Lord is in heaven. But until the life, death, and resurrection of Jesus there was no way of knowing if it was possible to join God in his home. Indeed, many were not sure that life existed beyond the grave let alone in heaven.

In the Upper Room, the night before his death, Jesus laid any uncertainty to rest. "Do not let your hearts be troubled," he said to his disciples, "you believe in God; believe also in me. My Father's house has many rooms; if that were not so, would I have told you that I am going there to prepare a place for you? And if I go and prepare a place for you, I will come back and take you to be with me that you also may be where I am" (John 14:1–3). From that moment to this very day, Christians have believed that heaven is our home. Jesus' resurrection is our guarantee. His return, to take us home, is our hope. The window of heaven is open.

# HOME

## Jerusalem

Jerusalem is sacred to Jews, Muslims, and Christians. For Jews it is the ancestral capital, the location of the temple (now missing), and the *Kotel*—the Western Wall—the ultimate place of prayer. For Muslims it is the site of Muhammad's (dream) ascent to heaven, marked by the beautiful Dome of the Rock on Mount Moriah. And for Christians it is the epicenter of redemption, the city where Jesus died, rose again, and ascended to the Father. For me and my family, it is home.

We moved there in 1981 at the invitation of Israeli government officials. They suggested we plant an interdenominational, international church (this is a looong story for another book). It was an offer we couldn't refuse, so we resigned a church we had planted a few years previously north of Toronto and moved to Jerusalem. Our children were aged seven, five, and three. For the first month we lived in a hotel.

After a lot of searching we found and leased a new flat in an old residential neighborhood called Rehavia. The streets were narrow and shaded with multilayered residences behind the hedges and trees. It was peaceful, historic, and to our surprise right on the border with an ultra-orthodox Jewish community. We learned a lot about Sabbath culture (barriers on the streets from Friday evening to Saturday evening, automatic Sabbath lighting systems that often malfunctioned, and then the quiet knocks at our door on Friday evenings asking for our seven-year-old to come over and turn on the lights, taking offence at my wife's blond hair and summer-weight sleeveless dresses, aggressive shouts of "Shabbas! Shabbas!" as we drove out the one barrier-free street).

Then there was furniture and appliances to be ordered—"That will be four months before delivery, *adoni* [sir]." Same thing with a car—four months before its arrival from Europe (at *twice* the price we'd pay in North America). Fortunately, we didn't have to wait eight years (!) for a phone—the flat came with one. And, to our chagrin, we had to pay the first year's lease in advance (this the result of my first Israeli negotiating experience—they had wanted *two* years in advance!).

My wife Kathy and I had been to Jerusalem a few times as visitors, but to walk around the city with our family as new residents was thrilling. Just the sight of the Old City walls elicited an excited response from our two boys. Even our daughter jumped from her stroller and ran over to slap her little hands against the ancient stones. The Jaffa Gate with people of every nation and fashion streaming in and out, David's Citadel towering above, the narrow stone-terraced David Street leading down through the *shouk*, the hawkers, the smells of roasting cashews, exotic spices, and the fragrance of thousands of years of human presence were intoxicating. The sesame-encrusted bagels with the accompanying newspaper-wrapped spices, the ice-cold drinks, the cries of beggars, the calls to prayer from the Muslim *muezzin* (via several minarets), the heat and the dust, were enthralling. We felt like we'd landed on a different planet. Just the thought that we now *lived* here was almost too much. We reveled in it.

The novelty was never to wear off. How can you get casual about Jerusalem? Can you ever take for granted a city with thousands of years of history, much of it at the epicenter of world interest? In the next seven years of living there we were only scratching the surface. But we did have to live. Thus, the adventure of grocery shopping in small *makolets* (tiny neighborhood corner stores), opening a bank account (after depositing all our money we were told there would be no checks till the following week—whaaat?!), finding a doctor, getting an Israeli driver's license, dealing with the phone company, registering our oldest son (seven years old) in a local school . . . all without Hebrew language skills. Talk about a baptism of fire! And, oh yes, I forgot to mention the lineups at the stores, banks, and government offices—actually *lineup* is a misnomer—try *scrums*. In Israel, the survival of the fittest is a core value.

The rhythms of Jerusalem beguiled us. Perhaps it was the constant stress of military engagement and threats on the borders, but Israelis know how to relax and socialize, some starting each morning with coffee and an *oogah* (*cake*—read croissant, muffin, bun) at a sidewalk cafe on the Ben Yehuda pedestrian mall in the center of Jerusalem, then another snacking and visiting break during the afternoon siesta between two and five in the afternoon, and a late-night dinner on their *mirpesset* (patio/balcony) in the cool of the evening. But the most alluring of all was (and which remains) the cadence of *Kabalat Shabat*: welcoming the Sabbath every Friday at sundown.

At about three on Friday afternoon you can almost hear Jerusalem exhale. Traffic thins to a virtual standstill and you see family groups walking to their parents' homes, flowers, challah bread, and wine in hand. By four-thirty pretty much everything is bathed in peace. You know that the *Shabbat* candles are about to be lit in each home. The siren sounds as the sun sets, and the Sabbath begins. All is at rest.

Within a year or so we transitioned from tourists to residents. Our children became fluent in Hebrew (as did Kathy) and I labored with language lessons. On Saturdays the kids had the run of the city, climbing trees, skateboarding, exploring the walls and rooftops of the Old City, rappelling with Israeli cadets on the cliffs of the Hinnom Valley, and in the midst of all this assimilation we founded what is now known as King of Kings Church (kkm.network).

We had worked ourselves out of a job within seven years, having positioned others to succeed us. To my joy the ministry is doing better without us than it was with us. There's no greater fulfillment for a trailblazer than to see a highway evolve from his efforts. Even though we now live in Canada, and our three pastor children have their own families and ministries, Jerusalem is still our home town.

Everyone, including rolling stones like us, needs a home. We look forward to the new Jerusalem.

## Window No. 3
## Prayer

### A Place for You

Our heavenly Father,
We pray with King Solomon
That you will "hear from heaven,
Your dwelling place."
Indeed, not just your place,
But as your Son promised his disciples,
"A place for you." Our place.
We are pilgrims
Seeking "a better country. . .
A heavenly home."
This world cannot contain us.
We are looking for a city,
A holy one,
The heavenly Jerusalem.
You are our God
In heaven above.
You are our home.
We long to take our place.
Until then we "press toward the mark"
Of your high calling
Hoping to hear you say one day
"Well done . . . enter in."

# Window No. 4
# Worship

> O ye Waters that be above the Firmament,
>     Bless ye the Lord . . .
> O ye showers and dew,
>     Bless ye the Lord: praise him,
>         And magnify him forever. . . . O let the earth
> Bless the Lord: yea, let it praise him,
>     and magnify him forever . . .
>
> —Morning prayer, *Book of Common Prayer*, 1662

In our Western world I suspect that we may have lost the depth of meaning when we pray, "Hallowed be thy name." The meaning of *hallowed* is *holy* or *sacred*. But for us, *holy* is a sort of religious designation only, not a deep description of the nature of God. You can be sure that when Jesus said *holy* it had far greater significance for his hearers than it does for us. Let's explore this a bit. Have your Bible at hand; we're going to look at a lot of Scripture:

> I am the Lord, your Holy One, Israel's Creator, your king. (Isa 43:15)

> For your Maker is your husband—The Lord Almighty is his name—the Holy One of Israel is your Redeemer; he is called the God of all the earth. (Isa 54:5)

> But the Lord Almighty will be exalted by his justice, and the holy God will be proved holy by his righteous acts. (Isa 5:16)

The essential meaning of "holy" (*kadosh*) is "apartness." The adjective *kadesh* describes anyone or anything sacred, as distinct from the "common" or "profane"(Hebrew *cool*). On the occasion of the burning bush in Exod 3, God warned Moses to keep his distance: "Do not come any closer" (*stay apart*). "Take off your sandals, for the place where you are standing is holy ground" (Exod 3:5). Then, when God declared "I am the God of your father, the God of Abraham, the God of Isaac and the God of Jacob," Moses turned away, "because he was afraid to look at God" (Exod 3:6).

The fact that the Lord chose to speak to Moses from a burning bush is significant. Holiness as fire characterizes many of the theophanies of the Old Testament. Mount Sinai is an excellent example:

> Mount Sinai was covered with smoke, because the Lord descended on it in fire. The smoke billowed up from it like smoke from a furnace, and the whole mountain trembled violently. (Exod 19:18)
>
> To the Israelites the glory of the Lord looked like a consuming fire on top of the mountain. (Exod 24:17)
>
> Then the Lord spoke to you out of the fire. You heard the sound of words but saw no form. (Deut 4:12)
>
> For the Lord your God is a consuming fire, a jealous God. (Deut 4:24)

Then in Deut 5 we read:

> 23. When you heard the voice out of the darkness, while the mountain was ablaze with fire, all the leaders of your tribes and elders came to me.
>
> 24. And you said, "The Lord our God has shown us his glory and his majesty, and we have heard his voice from the fire. . . .
>
> 25. This great fire will consume us, and we will die if we hear the voice of the Lord our God any longer.

26. For what mortal has ever heard the voice of the living God speaking out of fire, as we have, and survived?"

Long after this encounter, King David wrote, "Smoke rose from his nostrils; consuming fire came from his mouth, burning coals blazed out of it" (Ps 18:8; see 2 Sam 22:9–15).

Isaiah saw the future "Day of the Lord" in these fiery terms as well (Isa 34):

8. For the Lord has a day of vengeance, a year of retribution, to uphold Zion's cause.
9. Edom's streams will be turned into pitch, her dust into burning Sulphur; her land will become blazing pitch!
10. It will not be quenched night or day; its smoke will rise forever.

Fire imagery is employed frequently as God's holiness is described by the prophets. Nouns such as *light, heat, smoke, flame, coals, furnace, caldron, ashes,* and *brimstone* are often matched with verbs like *scorch, blaze, consume, burn, kindle, glow, warm,* and *quench.* Even the angelic seraphim who cry "Holy, Holy, Holy" are *the fiery ones* (*seraph*—to burn).

The last of the Old Testament era prophets was Jesus' cousin, John the Baptist. As he preached his firebrand message from the wilderness, baptizing penitents in the Jordan River, he boldly declared, "I baptize you with water for repentance. But after me comes one who is more powerful than I. . . . He will baptize you with the Holy Spirit and fire" (Matt 3:11). A year or so later, Jesus himself said, "I have come to bring fire on earth, and how I wish it were already kindled!" (Luke 12:49). A few decades after Jesus' death and resurrection, the anonymous writer to the Hebrews stated, "Our God is a consuming fire" (Heb 12:29), which of course was the point: fire consumes. It refines. Our natural reflex is to stay away.

In Deuteronomy we read, "God is a consuming fire, a jealous God" (4:24). Fire and jealousy are concomitant in his holiness. Jealousy has a negative connotation, which is not necessarily the case in that it can be *jealousy of,* but can also be *jealousy for,* one reactive the other proactive. In the Greek it is derived from a root *to boil*, while in Hebrew the nuance is *to become red in the face*. Jealousy is hot.

*Hot* as in *focused single-mindedness*. When experienced selfishly it produces hatred or envy, but when directed to others it produces zealous selflessness, as in "I am jealous for your future" or "I am jealous for your well-being" or "I want the best for you." Any parent can relate to this proactive emotion. Indeed, jealousy and passion go hand in hand. It's hot, not cold or lukewarm. As the object of a parent's jealousy for his/her future, the child feels the heat. It sometimes creates a fight-or-flight reaction. This may be why the apostle Paul wrote, "And you, fathers, provoke not your children to wrath" (Eph 6:4 KJV).

Idolatry on Israel's part always provoked the wrath of God. He was jealous for his divine prerogatives and for Israel's well-being. There is any number of Scriptural references. Here are a few:

> They made him jealous with their foreign gods and angered him with their detestable idols. (Deut 32:16)

> They angered him with their high places; they aroused his jealousy with their idols. (Ps 78:58)

> The Spirit lifted me up between earth and heaven and in visions of God he took me to Jerusalem, to the entrance of the north gate of the inner court, where the idol that provokes to jealousy stood. (Ezek 8:3)

> Judah did evil in the eyes of the Lord. By the sins they committed they stirred up his jealous anger. (1 Kgs 14:22)

The Lord had no patience for covenant breaking. He demanded total covenantal fealty:

> The Lord will never be willing to forgive them; his wrath and zeal will burn against them. All the curses written in this book will fall on them, and the Lord will blot out their names from under heaven. (Deut 29:20)

> Neither their silver nor their gold will be able to save them on the day of the Lord's wrath. In the fire of his jealousy the whole earth will be consumed. (Zeph 1:18)

Jeremiah, "the weeping prophet," mitigated these harsh words with a word of hope to the disobedient: "And if that nation I warned repents of its evil, then I will relent and not inflict on it the disaster I had planned" (Jer 18:8). Fortunately, for the contrite, "The Lord is merciful and gracious, slow to anger, and abounding in mercy" (Ps 103:8 KJV). And in Ps 103:9 we read, "He will not always strive with us, nor will he keep his anger forever."

You may have heard or read a term coined by a German theologian in his book *The Idea of the Holy*: *mysterium tremendum*. Rudolph Otto wanted to express the suprarational experience human beings sometimes have when in the presence of the *holy* or *numinous*. It is both *tremendous* (terrifying) and *fascinous* (fascinating). God's holiness evokes both fear and awe. Perhaps this is why King Solomon wrote, "The fear of the Lord is the beginning of wisdom, and the knowledge of the Holy One is understanding" (Prov 9:10 KJV). Even as we turn our eyes away from the burning bush, we are drawn to its light and warmth. We stand close enough to hear the Lord tell us his name with the promise, "I will be with you" (Exod 3:1–15).

To Jesus' Jewish audience the Lord's name was unspeakable, literally. In response to Moses' question at the burning bush God had answered, "I Am" or "I Am Who I Am" or "I Will Be Who I Will Be" (YHWH—*Yahweh*—Heb). But that name was not to be pronounced. To do so was to invoke God's very presence, a holy presence too fearful for words, in which one could not live. So, over the centuries whenever the Jews spoke or read God's name they would say *Adonai* (my Lord) and, in conversation would call him *ha Shem* (the Name). Even in writing, an orthodox Jew today will refer to the Lord as G-D. The Name is ineffable. Its authority, power, and holiness must be revered.

Later, when Moses was leading the children of Israel through forty years of wilderness wanderings, the Lord said, "See, I am sending an angel ahead of you to guard you along the way and to bring you to the land I have prepared. Pay attention to him and listen to what he says. Do not rebel against him; he will not forgive your rebellion, since my Name is in him" (Exod 23:20–21). The

Name was Israel's Champion. This was why the Name was not to be exploited for personal gain (Exod 20:7). Authority accompanied the Name, as did blessings and curses, and faithful prayer. And what was the bottom line of Aaron's priestly blessing?

> The Lord bless you and keep you;
> The Lord make his face shine upon you,
> And be gracious to you.
> The Lord lift up his countenance upon you,
> And give you peace.

Was it peace (shalom)? Grace? Presence? Yes, all the above, but the purpose was: "So they shall put my name on the children of Israel" (Num 6:24–27).

God's name was the incorporation of his person. His love for Israel had seen him bearing them out of four hundred years of slavery in Egypt "on eagles' wings" with a fatherly call to "obey my voice and keep my covenant." They would be "a special treasure. . . . a kingdom of priests and a holy nation" (Exod 19:4–6). They would be the personification of the Name.

In Jesus' day the faith of Israel was predicated, as it had always been, on the revelation of God's name. However much ideology, religious piety, and cultural core values might spring up over time, the pivot point of Jewishness was the Name. In Ps 9:10 we read, "Those who know your name trust in you, for you, Lord, have never forsaken those who seek you." And in Ps 91:14: "Because he loves me . . . I will rescue him; I will protect him, for he acknowledges my name."

So, in his priestly prayer for the disciples in the Upper Room, the night before his death, Jesus *hallowed* the Name by declaring to his Father, "I have manifested thy name" (John 17:6, 26 KJV). As the personification of Israel he had revealed the very character and purpose of God.

One must tread lightly when praying "hallowed be thy name." The point of worship is to ascribe worth (*worth-ship*) to the Holy One of Israel. It's not about us, but all about him. The Name is the Holy of Holies.

WORSHIP

## King of Kings

We had moved to Jerusalem in 1981 at the invitation of Israeli government officials who had encouraged us to start an international church. After eighteen months of adjustment and enculturation we were ready. But how does one start a church? Especially in the city where the very first church began?

During those formative months I had been engaged in three projects: *Kibbutz Shalom*—a short-term program I had created for North American young adults to do volunteer work on Israeli *kibbutzim*; *Campus Shalom*—a Christian chaplaincy ministry I started on the campus of the Hebrew University in Jerusalem; and weekly broadcasting shifts in Southern Lebanon with the *Voice of Hope*, a Christian radio station located in a war zone just north of the Israeli border town of Metula. Both *Kibbutz Shalom* and *Campus Shalom* had required a lot of behind-closed-doors conversations (sometimes interrogations) with various officials.

The basic question was "Why?" Why did I want to bring volunteers to Israel's *kibbutzim*? Didn't I know that some of the border *kibbutzim* were often under fire from the Palestine Liberation Organization? Why did I want to start a chaplaincy program at the Hebrew University? A Christian chaplain at the world's largest Jewish university? What's up with that? They pushed, and I pushed back (Israelis respect and respond to confrontation). The weekly drives into South Lebanon met with not just a "Why?" but also with a "Whaat?!" *Mishugah* ("crazy")! A young man with a young family should *not* risk Katyusha rockets, mortars, and tank battles! Even our neighbors joined the disapprobation. But the northern border *kibbutzim*, the Jewish university, and the rocket fire in Lebanon were all part of an equation providing track record, integrity, and faithful commitment to Israel that would prove to be foundational to navigating future obstacles in planting a church in Jerusalem.

And there *were* obstacles. Within our first two months we had been interviewed under pretext by a journalist who published an article in the leading Israeli women's magazine calling us Israel's "newest threat." The ultra-orthodox, anti-missionary organization, *Yad L'Achim* (Hand of the Brothers) began surveillance and built a file on us, and even Jerusalem's Christian ministerial told us to go home: "All you're going to do is dilute the soup. The most people you can hope for in a congregation is fifteen or twenty." None of this fazed us, of course. We were pursuing a calling. I had no plan, no strategy. My only agenda was to hold on to the Father's hand, walk in his shadow, and go through the doors he opened. Dependence and obedience go hand in hand.

In August of 1983 we held our first service in a small apartment owned by a local Israeli pastor. It was an inauspicious beginning. Our congregation was comprised of our family of five and twelve students from our Campus Shalom ministry. There was not one Israeli in the group, and the only one fluent in Hebrew was our nine-year-old son, Todd. We called ourselves (somewhat presumptuously) "Jerusalem Christian Assembly." My pulpit was a stack of Bibles on a coffee table. I preached on the account in Acts 2 where Luke describes the birth of the church. My text was the forty-second verse: "And they continued steadfastly in the apostles' doctrine and fellowship, in the breaking of bread, and in prayers." As I saw it then and still see it, the sustainability of the early church pivoted on biblical teaching, social interaction, and prayerful resolution. The application: we're planting a seed today that will need a lot of this kind of nurturing to survive and thrive. Some forty years later King of Kings Assembly, the renamed Jerusalem Christian Assembly, is a mighty oak (thanks to the Lord, and in no small part to the faithfulness of our successors, Wayne and Ann Hilsden).

In 1 Chr 16:4 the Chronicler describes King David's appointing of priests and Levites to minister before the newly placed ark of the covenant in "the tabernacle . . . erected for it." They were to "invoke, thank and praise the Lord God of Israel." This is what we endeavored to do in our new Jerusalem church.

The congregation, growing from week to week, quickly learned that this baby church was founded in worship. "Hallowed be thy name" was our signature. Every service we invited (*invoked*) the Lord to be present, we expressed our gratitude in prayer and expository preaching, and we praised and praised some more in beautiful Hebrew lyrics and inspired indigenous music. It was, and is, the place to be on a Jerusalem Sunday evening. At King of Kings, the window of worship is wide open for entry by the hallowed King of kings.

## Window No.4
## Prayer

Holy, Holy, Holy

In you O Lord
We put our trust.
You have never forsaken us
Because you love us.
And we will never forsake you
Because we love you.
You are steadfast in love
And mercy,
Patient and slow to anger.
Yet your jealousy for our best
Is a fearful thing.
Your holy anger will not tolerate
Those who worship their own gods,
Nor will you turn a blind eye
To those who blaspheme your Name.
You are holy, apart
Even while you are near.
Were it not for the mystery of your grace
We would be lost.
We thank you that the
Gift of salvation in Christ
Has enabled us to approach
Your unapproachable light.
Holy, Holy, Holy
Is your Name.

## Window No. 5
# Humility

> Humility is only doubt
> And does the sun and moon blot out
> Rooting over with thorns and stems
> The buried soul and all its gems
> This life's dim windows of the soul
> Distorts the heavens from pole to pole
> And leads you to believe a lie
> When you see with, not through, the eye.
>
> —*The Everlasting Gospel*, William Blake, 1818

Seeing "through the eye," as Blake put it, reflects the biblical assertion that "we walk by faith, not by sight" (2 Cor 5:7). Only faith can assure us that it is *thy name*, not ours, that is to be lifted high. If that faith is lacking we pursue our own agenda, *ascribing worth* to status and power in order to affirm the belief that *we* control our lives. Independence is our goal; dependence is to be avoided. Humility is for losers.

Nevertheless, the Lord's Prayer sets the tone right from the top. It is "thy name"—the Father's name—that is to be "hallowed." And as we'll see, it is "thy kingdom" and "thy will" that are prioritized. In the latter part of the prayer we are supplicants (*humble petitioners*), wholly dependent ones acknowledging our lowly status in the presence of the Holy One. He is in heaven and we are on earth (Eccl 5:2), so be humble or go home . . . "let your words be few."

Another English poet, Samuel Taylor Coleridge in "The Devil's Thoughts," wrote: "And the Devil did grin, for his darling sin/Is pride that apes humility."[1]

One cannot discuss humility without discussing pride. They are polarities for sure, but sometimes one can encroach on the other. Both require some thought. Let's start with pride.

In the Bible, pride is seen as self-glorification and presumption. It is *ground zero* in sin: Isaiah 2:6–22 captures God's abhorrence to its arrogance. I quote verses 11, 12, and 22:

> 11. The eyes of the arrogant will be humbled, and human pride brought low; the Lord alone will be exalted in that day.
>
> 12. The Lord Almighty has a day in store for all the proud and lofty, for all that is exalted (and they will be humbled). . . .
>
> 22. Stop trusting in mere humans, who have but a breath in their nostrils. Why hold them in esteem?

The prophet Amos put it bluntly: "The Lord God Almighty declares, 'I abhor the pride of Jacob'" (Amos 6:8). Obadiah warns, "The pride of your heart has deceived you. . . . Though you soar like the eagle and make your nest among the stars, from there I will bring you down, says the Lord" (Obad 3, 4). And King David says succinctly, "The arrogant cannot stand in your presence" (Ps 5:5).

God's holiness and our pride are mutually exclusive. Holiness is his *apartness*, pride is ours. There is a "great gulf fixed" (Luke 16:26 KJV) between the two. Heaven is barred to the proud. When, however, we hallow "thy" name and not "my" name, the

---

1. Samuel Taylor Coleridge and Robert Southey, "The Devil's Thoughts" (Sep 7, 1799), https://romantic-circles.org/editions/shelley/devil/devil.stc1799.html.

gates swing open. This is because the Lord reserves the right to be exclusively glorified and exalted. He alone is worthy.

> Thou art worthy, O Lord, to receive glory and honor and power: for thou hast created all things and for thy pleasure they are and were created. (Rev 4:11 KJV)
>
> There is no one holy like the Lord; there is no one beside you; there is no Rock like our God. (1 Sam 2:2)
>
> Do not keep talking so proudly or let your mouth speak such arrogance, for the Lord is a God who knows, and by him deeds are weighed. (1 Sam 2:3)

Pride should not be confused with mere ego. Ego is vanity and empty conceit. Pride on the other hand is self-divinification, a setting up of oneself on the throne. Pride sees any other god as rival. Independence is king.

The polar opposite of pride is humility. The noun appears only three times in the Old Testament (Prov 15:33; 18:12; 22:4) where it is described as coming "before honor" and as equivalent to "the fear of the Lord." The adjective *humble*, usually meaning *poor* or *afflicted*, is very common, seeing the humbled as "brought low" or "bowed down." In the New Testament it is often rendered as "lowliness" or "lowliness of mind." But, in the Bible, generally, humility is seen as the bedrock of righteousness which is being in right relationship with God. Deuteronomy 8, verses two and three, captures it: "Remember how the Lord your God led you all the way in the wilderness these forty years, to humble and test you in order to know what was in your heart, whether or not you would keep his commands. He humbled you, causing you to hunger and then feeding you with manna, which neither you nor your ancestors had known, to teach you that man does not live on bread alone but on every word that comes from the mouth of the Lord."

Then, centuries later, the prophet Micah distilled the bottom line of God's expectations with regard to his people: "He hath shewed thee, O man, what is good; and what doth the Lord require of thee but to do justly and to love mercy, and to walk humbly with thy God" (Mic 6:8 KJV).

The core values of a child of God are definitively described: righteousness, justice, mercy, and humility. "The high and lofty One, whose name is holy" dwells in the hearts of the humble (Isa 57:15; 66:2). The humble soul worships the Lord in a posture of meekness and poverty of spirit. Personal agendas are eclipsed by the person, the plan, and the presence of the Name. The light of the numinous floods in.

There really is no other choice when we open the window on the *thou-ness* of God. We mere creatures can exalt ourselves to the max fooling others (and mostly ourselves) but not the Almighty. "Strutting and fretting our hour upon the stage," as Shakespeare put it, comes to a blunt stop in the presence of our Creator. We are struck dumb. We have nothing to say. And if we're honest, we lament with Isaiah: "Woe is me for I am undone!" (Isa 6:5). Our only entry card is our poverty of spirit.

# Humility

## Joe

If Joe Burnham were alive today, he'd be on the street. I was five years old when I met him. He used to visit my dad every week in our home in Kelvington, Saskatchewan. He didn't attend Dad's little church of poor people. He felt he didn't belong. Poorer than the poor, marginalized by our town's citizenry, treated like a stray dog by his two spinster sisters, he was walking humility. Brought low by life he was the epitome of the downtrodden.

Joe was a fixture in our town, riding an ancient bicycle with rags stuffed in the tires (he couldn't afford tubes), wearing a World War II leather flying helmet, making spit-flecked motor noises with his cracked lips. Another town stray was often seen running alongside Joe as he rode—my dad dubbed this long-haired black mongrel "Smoky Stover." Other than Dad, Smoky was the only living being that treated Joe like a person. His sisters certainly didn't. Severe, forbidding-looking women clothed in long, black dresses, they wouldn't allow Joe into their house. They did, however, allow him to live in the adjacent shed where they fed him with scraps served in a metal bowl. At night he slept between two rank cotton mattresses (we called them "ticks"). Sometimes in the cold of winter Smoky would join him. They kept each other from freezing. Sometimes they would eat out of the same bowl.

Once a week (mostly Mondays) there would be a knock at our screened back door. I'd usually answer it—and there was Joe. "Hello Jimmy!" he'd say in his hollow voice, "Here, have some gum." And out of his pocket he'd produce a linty, stale stick of Wrigley's gum (usually Juicy Fruit that had lost its juice). I'd dutifully apply it to my teeth while Joe entered the kitchen. "Hello Brother!" I'd hear him greet my dad. "Let's talk about the Lord!" They would sit in our sparingly furnished living room and the conversation would begin. I sat on the stairs, eager to hear them talk.

Most of the people in our town saw Joe as the town fool. He was not only slighted, but on occasion I saw children throw stones at him as he passed on his bike. He never retaliated. He kept his eyes ahead as though he were pursuing a far horizon. Besides, he had seen fire before—artillery fire in North Africa in the war. No one knew it (except my dad, who had also served in WWII), but Joe was a hero. He had almost died defending three of his fellow soldiers in a skirmish near Tripoli. He had sustained a head injury, was hospitalized for several weeks and survived. His brain, however, was forever altered. Thus the hollow voice, the sometimes vacant stare, and his childlike persona. But, brain damage or not, he had a heart for God.

As I look back at Joe I think I can see now what I couldn't see then: he didn't lack comprehension, but he was deficient in expression. Limited in vocabulary he spoke in blunt fashion with little use of adjectives, adverbs, or color. Small talk was a stretch for him. He got right to the point with seeming disregard for social niceties. Dad understood this, so after sitting down he and Joe would go right to it.

"Brother, Father loves us. He healed my back yesterday [no further description given] and I know he will heal Mrs. Davidson too [she was the general store owner who had just been taken to our four-room hospital for some reason]. I'm praying for the Morrisons [their five-year-old son had drowned two weeks previously in a slough outside town] and also for Mrs. Thompson [who had been injured in a farming accident]. So much sadness. Father loves the sad."

Joe didn't ask "Why?" nor did he focus on himself. He loved God and God's people. He made no distinction—*all* were God's people. His mission from his shed to the streets on his bicycle was prayer for the hurting. It didn't seem to occur to him that he had any pressing needs, so when he came to see my dad his concern was others and their need of heaven's intervention. He asked nothing from Dad because the Lord was the source of healing for the world. Joe himself was simply a servant. He was the most low-maintenance man in town. And, in my view, he was also the most godly.

They talked about a number of things, all with the physical and spiritual needs of the townspeople in focus. Dad, as the only full-time pastor, and Joe as the only all-time itinerant observer, were truly in touch with the pulse of the town. Between the two of them there was little overlooked in their prayers for God's people. And, when it came to prayer, a remarkable transformation would take place. Joe would raise his face to heaven and the vacant stare turned to shining focus. His voice would lose its hollow timbre and become clear and distinct. And suddenly as though his brain was set free he expressed his heart in flowing, descriptive words with depth of meaning. I remember being both amazed and impressed with the obvious (to me) miracle. Joe was God's man. And in a sense he was Dad's mentor. This world was not his home, nor were its concerns about him. Rather it was all about God.

Joe would always conclude his visit by laying his right hand on Dad's shoulder and praying for him. Then, as he left, he would say, "Soon, I'll be with Father!" A year after Dad took on the pastorate of a church in another town we heard that Joe had been found one winter's morning lying peacefully between his mattresses, Smoky Stover at his side. He had gone home.

## Window No. 5
## Prayer

### We Bow Down

O Lord, your majesty,
Like the heavens,
Is beyond us.
We cannot comprehend
Let alone grasp
The wonders of your being,
The infinite mysteries of your works.
We are brought low
At the mention of your Holy Name.
Yet, even as we bow down
Our spirits are lifted by your promise
That "you will never leave us
Nor forsake us."
You choose to stoop
So that we can rise.
This knowledge is too great for us.
All we can do is humbly affirm
Your lordship and our dependence.
You are in control,
We are not.
Submission our posture
Your mercy our hope.
Do with us
As you will.

## Window No. 6
# Accountability

> Praise my soul, the King of heaven;
> To his feet thy tribute bring.
> Ransomed, healed, restored, forgiven,
> Who like me his praise should sing?
>
> —From a hymn by Henry Francis Lyte, 1834

THE KINGDOM OF HEAVEN was a constant theme in Jesus' ministry. Sometimes called the "kingdom of God," it had a three-fold meaning for his hearers: the kingdom as an eternal reality distinct from any space/time creation; the kingdom as an earthly manifestation folded into religious teaching and practice; and the kingdom as a future, eschatological expectation. But, key to any concept of kingdom was kingship. There must be a king.

Jesus' contemporaries were familiar with rabbinic teaching about the kingdom of God. Submission to God's will and obedience to the law of Moses meant "taking upon oneself the Kingdom of Heaven" as Israel had done at Mount Sinai (Exod 19–20). Daily repetition of the "Great Sh'ma"—"Hear, o Israel: The Lord our God, the Lord is one" (Deut 6:4)—was regarded as "taking upon oneself the *yoke* of the kingdom of God." Any observant Jew faithfully carried that burden. Over centuries of war occupation by foreign powers, and the day-to-day struggles of survival in the sandbox of

Palestine, that burden had become the yoke of hope for national deliverance. The heavenlies became a mere backdrop to earthly regency. They wanted a throne to be established in Jerusalem. They wanted the messiah to make his entry. So, when John the Baptist preached, "Repent, for the kingdom of heaven is at hand" (Matt 3:2 KJV), the people flocked to the Jordan in droves.

This predominantly eschatological emphasis on the kingdom was challenged by the concept of the *here but not yet* teaching of Jesus. Even as the day of the Lord was future, the kingdom of heaven was present in Jesus himself: "The Kingdom of God is in your midst" (Luke 17:21). This, of course, was generally beyond comprehension. How could Jesus be the personification of the kingdom?

Nevertheless, Jesus kept emphasizing his pivotal role in the kingdom. On one occasion when some of the crowd attributed his power over demons to be evidence that he himself was a sort of super demon he pushed back by saying, "Any kingdom divided against itself . . . will fall" (Luke 11:17). Then he declared his ease in dealing with mere petty demonic forces in stating, "If I drive out demons by the finger of God, then the Kingdom of God has come upon you" (Luke 11:14–20). So in this context "thy kingdom come" meant "thy kingdom *has* come upon us."

The "not yet" aspect of the kingdom was evident in Jesus' parables. There are many, but here are a few examples:

> This is what the Kingdom of God is like. A man scatters seed on the ground. Night and day, whether he sleeps or gets up, the seed sprouts and grows, though he does not know how. All by itself the soil produces grain . . . he puts the sickle to it, because the harvest has come. (Mark 4:26–29)

> What is the Kingdom of God like? What shall I compare it to? It is like a mustard seed, which a man took and planted in his garden. It grew and became a tree, and the birds perched in its branches. (Luke 13:18,19)

> What shall I compare the Kingdom of God to? It is like yeast that a woman took and mixed into about sixty

pounds of flour until it worked all through the dough. (Luke 13:20,21)

These planting and baking similes were about the gradual but inexorable natural process of growth. Jesus' ministry *was* the kingdom, both as seed and as the promise of consummation. The kingdom of God was both present and at the door. The nations would soon "perch in its branches." And it would be "the consolation of Israel" (Luke 2:25).

The prophet Isaiah had described the kingdom ideal (Isa 11):

1. A shoot will come up from the stump of Jesse; from his roots a Branch will bear fruit.
2. The Spirit of the Lord will rest on him—the Spirit of wisdom and of understanding, the Spirit of counsel and of might, the Spirit of the knowledge and fear of the Lord—and he will delight in the fear of the Lord.
3. He will not judge by what he sees with his eyes, or decide by what he hears with his ears; but with righteousness he will judge the needy, with justice he will give decisions for the poor of the earth.
4. He will strike the earth with the rod of his mouth; with the breath of his lips he will slay the wicked.
5. Righteousness will be his belt and faithfulness the sash around his waist.
6. The wolf will live with the lamb, the leopard will lie down with the goat, the calf and the lion and the yearling together; and a little child will lead them.

This kingdom has a king called the "Branch." He is Messiah, the "servant" of the Holy One of Israel: "Here is my servant, whom I uphold, my chosen one in whom I delight; I will put my spirit on him, and he will bring justice to the nations" (Isa 42:1).

The people had heard their rabbis say that mention of the kingdom *must* be made in all prayers, or it was no prayer. They were overstating it, but there's no doubt Jesus hit a nerve when he prayed, "Thy kingdom come." It resonated with King David's ancient declaration: "The Lord has established his throne in heaven, and his kingdom rules over all" (Ps 103:19).

The challenge for the people was their unfamiliarity with kingship and kingdom. There had not been a king over Israel and Judah for half a millennium. All they had now was foreign occupation with the rule of emperors and their proconsular despots (like Pilate). For most, the kingdom of God was a fantasy. But, it was not yet dead. The messianic hope was like "a bruised reed" and a "smoking flax" (Isa 42:3). They were down, but not out.

*Kingdom*, of course, implies rule, obedience, and accountability, all three implications incompatible with our secular world. "We serve no sovereign here" was the slogan of the American War of Independence. That principle is universal in all democratic republics. It has become a core cultural value for free people. So there is an inherent disconnect when we pray "thy kingdom come." Submission doesn't suit us.

But submission is more than mere acquiescence. Submission is about both authority and values. We may rebel when we're expected to submit to authority, but we easily, as conformists, submit to societal values. We want to be seen as both independent and in fashion. So, we may resist the king but we meld with the crowd. We "cherry pick" our resignations. Anything to avoid prioritizing accountability.

How familiar are we with concepts of kingdom and kingship? We watch the crown placed on the head of Charles III, but what if anything does that mean for us as individuals? The difference is Charles III exists in a secular world; God exists in an eternal world. We may choose to reject submission to a secular king, but as a subject of Christ we are not bound by things but instead are free. Jesus put it this way: "Therefore if the Son makes you free you are free indeed" (John 8:36 KJV). It's the open window of liberty.

## Accountability
## The Machete

I often say "I cut my teeth on a church pew." This statement is facetious but it does reflect the fact that I'm a churchman. I was born and bred for the ministry. I grew up under my dad's preaching with occasional sermons from visiting Bible teachers, missionaries, and evangelists. There was a common theme from the pulpit: Jesus is coming soon! It didn't matter if it was Christmas, Easter, weddings, or funerals; it seemed the preacher always got to the "second coming." The world is falling apart (this after the Second World War) and the kingdom of heaven is our only hope. Make way for the king! For sure he'll be here before 1956! As a preteen, especially during thunderstorms, I was always looking up. Jesus might be in those clouds! For dad's little congregation of prairie farmers this was more than "the hope of the church" (from the Greek *parousia*), it was an expectation.

The prevalent prairies poverty combined with belief in the imminent return of Jesus produced a predictable approach to building churches, summer church camps, and educational facilities: find it or build it cheap, and do it quickly! There is no time to waste. Evangelize the world before it's too late! Urgency prevailed.

This dire necessity of reaching the spiritually lost brought with it the call to pay the price. Personal comfort and interests were eclipsed by the big picture: "Rescue the perishing care for the dying . . ." was sung with fervency. "Where he leads me, I will follow . . ." We'd "go with him, with him, all the way." So a wave of young inexperienced messengers of the gospel committed themselves to planting and/or pastoring struggling little churches, or sailing overseas to unreached people groups, or itinerating from town to town—all without any promise of compensation other than to hear the Lord one day say, "Well done good and faithful servant." Indeed poverty was seen as the companion of mission. As was sacrifice and risk. When you're living for something bigger than yourself you're even willing to die for it. And many did.

I didn't realize it in my childhood, but I was being inculcated with a countercultural worldview. Instead of looking out for myself, I was to look out for Christ. His kingdom, not ours, was our chief concern, and he was king. I was to obey his leading without personal agendas and be accountable for my choices. I had, as the rabbis of Israel put it, "taken on myself the yoke of the kingdom of God." Even as a warm-blooded teenager I was aware of its weight. I was living beneath the ever present "shadow of his wings"—which brings me to the machete.

While pastoring in British Columbia in the late 1990s, I was exposed to the ravages of HIV and AIDS in East Vancouver. As I got our church involved in reaching out to the skeletal victims (mainly impoverished aboriginal sex workers), I had to confront this pandemic. Research made me aware that HIV and AIDS was/is the biggest orphan and widow maker in history. The greatest impact at that time was in sub-Saharan Africa. In Kwazulu Natal alone (southeast South Africa), the prevalence rate of this incurable disease was over 30 percent. The death toll was staggering. An entire generation of young adults was being wiped out.

King David's words in Ps 68:5 (KJV) struck me to the core: "A father to the fatherless, a defender of widows is God in his holy habitation." It was as though this ancient king was speaking directly to me. I had to do something about the orphans and young widows victimized by this global plague. So I resigned our great church and for the next eight months my wife and I lived out of suitcases. We started from scratch, laying the foundations for what is now, twenty-three years later (at time of writing) wowmission.com. ("WOW"—Working for Orphans and Widows). It has been/is a *huge* adventure.

One day we were driving with a few key leaders to a remote rural village in the African nation of Malawi. We had to pass through a few small towns on the way where there was a great deal of unrest due to a recent federal election that had been compromised by vote rigging. The first two showed signs of earlier protests: stones and small rocks on the road, a few smoldering truck tires, angry faces from the roadside market, but no current violence. The next town was in the midst of it. As we approached, we saw the smoke from the tire fires and several hundreds of mostly young men milling about. When we were within range they began throwing stones at us, and before we could escape we were suddenly surrounded by the shouting mob. Some of them tried to run the car over while others pounded on the doors and fenders. Then one of the young men rammed his hand against the passenger window, demanding I roll it down and give him money. In his other hand, he brandished a machete. For farmers a machete is an effective grass-cutting tool; for angry young men, it is a broadsword for slashing off hands and heads. I quickly pulled out all the money I had—about five dollars in Malawian kwacha. This wasn't enough. He demanded more. I saw his grip tighten on the machete.

Suddenly, I remembered Peter and John's response to the lame man at the temple gate: "Silver and gold have I none; but such as I have give I thee . . ." (Acts 3:6 KJV). Looking the young man in the eye (his face was six inches from mine), I said, "I know why you're angry, but a few kwacha are not the answer. I've given you all I have. But I can give you something else. Do you have a family?"

"Ya-ya . . . yes sir," he answered.

"Well, I'm a pastor, and I'd like to pray for them and for you. That okay?"

"Yes. You a pastor?" The machete dropped to his side.

I prayed for him, a brief prayer for his family's protection. He thanked me, turned to the mob, said something in their language (Chichewa), and the crowd parted to either side of the road. Then we were off. It took a few miles for the adrenaline rush to subside.

The "yoke of the kingdom" that we had taken upon ourselves was a machete that day. We didn't die but we had to be prepared to die. Why? Because "thy kingdom come" means exactly that.

## Window No. 6
## Prayer

### Repentance

You O Lord are King of kings,
Your kingdom eternal
And everlasting.
You have called us
To take on the "yoke"
And we have done so
Willingly.
But we are not so willing
To give account.
We still default to our need
For independence, our compulsion to control.
We want to be our own source
And beginning,
Our own final court of appeal.
Yet your love for us
And our love for you
Temper our self-absorption.
Righteousness and justice—the
Hallmarks of your kingdom,
Are infused within us by your Spirit.
And so we turn from our evil ways
To walk the narrow path
To your throne.

## Window No. 7
# Purpose

> The Immanent Will that stirs
> and urges everything...
>
> —Thomas Hardy, "Convergence of the Twain,"
> 1914

The prophet Zechariah captured both "hallowed be thy name" and "thy kingdom come" when he wrote, "The Lord will be king over the whole earth. On that day there will be one Lord, and his name the only name" (Zech 14:9). This sovereign is no figurehead. He is holy, just, and loving—with a plan and a purpose for his creation. He is not to be taken lightly. His will must be done. Indeed, his will *be* done.

And what is his will? To answer I think we need to go back to a watershed story in the book of Genesis. There we'll discover the will of the Lord in terms of "the way of the Lord." To do his will we must purpose to walk in his way. Take a look at Gen 18:1–20.

This is an account of what is called a *theophany*, an *appearance of God*: "And the Lord appeared to Abraham near the great trees of Mamre . . ." (Gen 18:1). As he was sitting in the shade of a tent flap he looked out through the noontime heat waves and saw three strangers approaching. He ran and invited them to a meal. As the food was prepared, Abraham enjoyed a long conversation.

In the talk the narrator mixes pronouns for the mysterious visitors. Sometimes "I," sometimes "they," sometimes singular, sometimes plural, and sometimes "the Lord" are all used. Regardless, the men declare that in a year's time "I" will return and Sarah will have a son. Sarah, well past childbearing years, overheard the prophetic word and laughed to herself, "I'm worn out and Abraham is old"— in her mind this was an impossibility. (By the way, the Hebrew verb "to laugh" is *tsahaq*, the root of *Itshaq* or "Isaac".) After a brief interchange between Sarah and the Lord, the three got up to resume their walk to Sodom. Abraham accompanied them for a bit, and before he saw them off the Lord said, "Shall I conceal from Abraham what I am about to do? For Abraham will surely be a great and mighty nation, and all the nations of the earth will be blessed through him. For I have chosen him so that he will charge his sons and his household after him to keep the way of the Lord to do righteousness and justice" (vv. 17, 19).

It was God's will to unilaterally enter into a covenant relationship with Abraham: "I will make you into a great nation, and I will bless you, I will make your name great, and you will be a blessing. I will bless those who bless you, and whoever curses you I will curse; and all peoples on earth will be blessed through you" (Gen 12:2–3).

The covenant was entered into formally and it was now up to Abraham and his descendants to perform their part in this everlasting agreement. God's will for them was that they act righteously and justly. Righteousness and justice were the bar, and that standard informed the prophetic call to Israel throughout the centuries to come. It persists for all men and women of faith to this day.

In this story, *righteousness* is a translation of *tzadkah* (or *tzedeq*) and *justice* of *mishpat*. Sometimes *tzadkah* can be translated as either/or depending on the context. *Righteousness* refers to the fulfillment of the demands of relationship with God, and *justice* the demands of relationship with neighbor. Or, *righteousness* addresses the vertical demands and *justice* the horizontal, even as God's character and stated values are rooted in both.

## Purpose

There are scores of references to righteousness and justice in the Old Testament. Here are just a few: "Righteousness and justice are the foundation of your throne; love and faithfulness go before you" (Ps 89:14) and "I will make justice the measuring line and righteousness the plumb line" (Isa 28:17).

Note the polar opposite to the above: "God will stretch out over Edom the measuring line of chaos and the plumb line of desolation" (Isa 34:11).

Amos, the first prophet to declare his prophecies in writing, wrote: "But let justice roll on like a river, righteousness like a never-failing stream!" (Amos 5:24).

And Jeremiah wrote: "I am the Lord, who exercises kindness, justice and righteousness on earth, for in these I delight" (Jer 9:24).

Jesus restated these core values when challenged by a young scribe (legal expert) about the bottom line of God's expectation of the faithful (Mark 12):

> 28. One of the teachers of the law came and heard them debating. Noticing that Jesus had given them a good answer, he asked him, "Of all the commandments, which is the most important?"
>
> 29. "The most important one," answered Jesus, "is this. Hear, O Israel: The Lord our God, the Lord is one. Love the Lord your God with all your heart and with all your soul and with all your mind and with all your strength.
>
> 30. The second is this: Love your neighbor as yourself.
>
> 31. There is no commandment greater than these."[1]

Jesus hit the sweet spot of the prophetic call to Israel. God expects his people to be both righteous and just. And how does one fulfill this expectation? By *love* for both God and neighbor.

Theologians in past centuries used to refer to love as *disinterestedness*, meaning *unselfishness*. That is, when one loved God or

---

1. Matthew writes, "All the Law and the Prophets hang on these two commandments" (Matt 22:40), and Luke writes, "Do this and you will live" (Luke 10:28).

neighbor the object was to add value to the loved one rather than to gain value for oneself. Love was outward, not inward. But, they may have missed a crucial point. Yes, love meant to add value to God and neighbor, however, Jesus said we're to love ourselves as well. First God, then neighbor, then self—with *all* our "heart, soul, mind, and strength."

"Heart," of course, refers to our emotions. Love is lubricated by feeling even though it is sustained by choices. "Soul" and "mind" were seen by the rabbis as the intellect; the scribe rightly summarized "soul" and "mind" as *understanding* (Mark 12:33), and "strength" referred to *will* or *volition*. We're to love God, neighbor, and self with intellect, emotion, and will—our thinking, our feeling, and our choosing.

Jesus gave no motivational talk, nor did he delineate the *how to* of intellectual, emotional, and volitional love. He just said, "Do it." The finer points, the tactical process of fulfilling the overarching strategy of God's will, are left up to us as we're "led by the Spirit." This is where prayer makes its mark.

Yes, there is mystery in this thing called prayer. "Thy will be done on earth as it is in heaven" is a bold leap, an opening of a window that almost blinds the soul with its implications. The humbling wonder in the linkage between heaven and earth, the engagement of divine with human will, the inherent gap between the two bridged by a whisper, is almost too much to bear. But somehow, some way, the purpose is achieved as we submit our will to his where "the whole earth [is] filled with his glory" (Ps 72:19).

## Leaving the Dock

As a boy, I used to deliver *The Globe and Mail* newspaper to a suburb of Sudbury, Ontario, "the nickel capital of the world." In winter, it may have been *the freezer capital* with northern temperatures hovering in the minus-forty-degree range. Add wind and early morning darkness with aggressive neighborhood dogs, and one might wonder why a kid would do this for $2.20 a week.

A van would deliver a bale of newspapers every morning at five. The van door would slam shut (working like an alarm clock for me), the papers dropped at the end of our driveway, and I would quickly put on a coat and boots, bring the bale into the house, sort and collate (there were often advertising flyers in a separate bale), stuff everything into a canvas shoulder bag, and set out in the freezing air, my boots crunching on the frosty snow (the "caa-runch, caa-runch" echoing off the silent houses).

Two hours later I'd return, feet and hands numb, face red from the cold, shivering and ready for a bowl of hot oatmeal. Opening the side door to the house I'd look down the stairs to the basement and there as always was my father, walking back and forth in prayer. Sometimes I'd see him kneeling at a chair, his arms and head resting on his duct-tape repaired King James Bible. He'd been in prayer since 4:30 a.m. This was his rhythm. He was an early riser, and an early adapter to the beat of heaven. "Thy will be done" was the root of his spiritual DNA. He believed in following the Leader.

No one follows a leader who can't be trusted. And you don't trust someone you don't know. Dad trusted his Leader, even as he was "getting to know" (as he often said) the Lord by studying his word. He was quick to say there was more about God he didn't know than what he did know, but was committed to "growing in the grace and knowledge" of the Father. So he practiced what he knew, yet humbly acknowledged that "I've got a lot to learn." He was a pilgrim.

Pilgrims in history have often been visionaries and pioneers who set out not knowing their ultimate destination. It's as though they had a migratory urge, perhaps a compulsion, to pursue the far horizon. As in the book of Hebrews, "[they] went out not knowing where [they were] going" (Heb 11:8), their life choices were predicated on "a far country," and for them the joy was in the journey. The uncertainty of the path was eclipsed by the certainty of the upward call. Hope in the Father's will fueled their determination.

For many of us, however, hope is not enough. We want a blueprint, more books, more motivational retreats, more money, and more better. It's as though we are loading a ship at the dock with all the possible contingencies, to the point where it's beginning to sink with the weight. What's more, we need navigational charts and assurances of good weather. We're risk-averse, but we rationalize by saying, "I just want the *perfect* will of God," as if a true believer should not make a mistake. Meanwhile, the boat is dragging on the bottom.

At some point we've got to leave the dock. But what if I sail in the wrong direction? Kudos to you. If you sail in the wrong direction God can make a midcourse correction, but he can't do a thing with a ship that's not moving.

For Dad the upward call took precedence over personal preference. His agenda was under orders: God's will was all that mattered. He took a church with no regard for career moves or salary. Indeed, when being interviewed by a pulpit committee he didn't even think of asking what the compensation was to be. It was enough that God was leading him. God would supply his needs.

So how does one recognize "the upward call"? Then, how does one appropriate it? Dad would say you start with the Scriptures, "growing in the grace and knowledge of the Lord," doing so in concert with self-knowledge of the Lord, and in concert with self-awareness of personal gifting, tendencies, and comfort zone. When contacted by the search committee of a church looking to hire a pastor, the first question he would ask was, "What are you looking for in a pastor?" If the answer was "a strong administrator," he knew it wasn't for him. No need to seek the Lord on that one. Administrator he was not; he always delegated management to others. He was a preacher. The pulpit was his cockpit. He trusted his gifting and, as he often said, he stayed in his lane. Do what you're good at and leave it there.

When it comes to God's will and us there is a basic principle: he made us for a purpose. Only he knows what that purpose is. We don't know that purpose early in life. But there are more than enough clues for us to work it out over time. It starts with knowing our talents and giftings. Sometimes these qualities are evident from an early age, and sometimes it takes time to grow into them. The slightest leaning in childhood can become a major strength in adulthood. The key is to stay with it as it develops incrementally. For this to happen, we've got to "stay in our lane." The biblical call to righteousness and justice is a good place to start. Call it a path on which to grow into "the planting of the Lord." And we've got to remember that the Lord's will *is* a path, not a destination.

## Window No. 7
## Prayer

### The Greatest Commandment

We thank you our Father
For giving us your Son
Who taught us that the love of God,
Love of neighbor, and love of self
Were "all the law and the prophets".
"No commandment greater than these."
He said:
"Do this and you will live."
To love you is to fulfill righteousness,
And to love neighbor justice.
We admit that we often lack
The maturity to rise above self-interest.
We pray that you will help us
To engage our mind, emotion, and will
In rising above ourselves,
To see the bigger picture both in
Your interests and those of our neighbor.
Help us O Lord to be givers, not takers,
Contributors, not consumers.
May our core values reflect
Your call to love
Even as you are love.

## Window No. 8
# Simplicity

> Our life is frittered away by detail...
> Simplify, simplify!
>
> —HENRY DAVID THOREAU, *WALDEN*, 1854

ONE OF THE MOST fascinating stories from the Old Testament is the story of Hagar (Gen 16). She was an Egyptian slave girl owned by Abram's wife, Sarai. She may have been a third of Sarai's age. (Sarai was seventy-six.)

Sarai was barren and now well beyond childbearing years, whereas Hagar was in her prime. Barrenness was a great disgrace for women at that time, and Sarai's shame was all the greater in that her family's wanderings had been predicated on a promise Abram had received from God that he and Sarai were to parent "a great nation" (Gen 12:2). Frustrated and disappointed, she did what was commonly done in the ancient Near East—she gave Hagar to Abram as a surrogate. "Perhaps I can build a family through her."

Hagar was soon pregnant displaying her swelling form in Sarai's presence, making her mistress "look slight in her eyes" (in Hebrew, perhaps a play on words—*slight*, as in diminished or very unpregnant). Indignant and humiliated, Sarai began to abuse Hagar to the point that she ran away out into the wilderness of Beersheba on her way back to Egypt via the *Way of Shur*. Her plight was desperate: a pregnant young woman, alone, without food or shelter from the searing heat. She found a spring and stopped. "At least I won't die of thirst," she may have thought, "while I wait for a trade caravan to rescue me."

Suddenly "the angel of the Lord" appeared and said, "return to your mistress and suffer abuse at her hand." Before Hagar could respond, he went on to tell her that the son she was bearing would be the father of a multitude "beyond counting" and that she should name him "Ishmael" (in Hebrew, *God has heard*).

Hagar, who thought this messenger was God himself, amazed that she was still alive (the Hebrew view was that seeing God meant instant death), referred to the Lord as "El-Roi" (*God who sees me*). She went back to Sarai and gave birth. Abram called the son Ishmael. He was now a father at eighty-six years of age.

The name Hagar gave to the angel, *God who sees*, became bedrock in the biblical view of the attributes of God. In various iterations it morphed into what theologians call "providence," from the Latin *providere* ("to foresee") and from the Greek *pronoi* ("forethought"). Out of his eternal present the Lord sees (omniscience) and provides (providence). The universe is dependent on his constant presence (immanence) and is preserved by his faithful provisions (providence). Indeed, the holiness and providence of God are fundamental to everything he is and does—which takes us back to the Lord's Prayer . . .

When we pray "Give us this day our daily bread," we're appealing to God's providence. A window in our soul opens to the "steadfast love of the Lord" which "never ceases"; "his mercies never come to an end; they are new every morning; great is your faithfulness" (Lam 3:22–23).

The Lord "knows what you need before you ask him" (Matt 6:8). Our daily bread is a given. He is *the God who sees.*

Because he sees past, present, and future, we don't have to. "Therefore do not worry about tomorrow, for tomorrow will worry about itself," Jesus said just a few minutes after the Lord's Prayer (Matt 6:34). Why borrow trouble from the future? Worry is a nonstarter that can erode your soul.

"Daily bread" means food security. It's not just bread for now—it's bread for tomorrow and after. A provident heavenly Father will not see the children of the righteous "begging bread" (Ps 37:25). He will not withhold good things his children ask of him (Ps 84:11). This is why Jesus discouraged his disciples from reliance on material things. "Do not store up for yourselves treasures on earth, where moths and vermin destroy, and where thieves break in and steal" (Matt 6:19). He emphasized the unfailing security stored up in heaven (Matt 6:20), the place where God provides and manages sustainable treasure. Providence frees us to serve God, not money (Matt 6:24). And we serve him by prioritizing "his kingdom and his righteousness." When we do, material provision is a no-brainer (Matt 6:33).

So keep your "needs" simple. Material abundance is no match for a provident heavenly Father. His pockets are deep. We don't have to buffer our lives with the *what-ifs* of the future. Anxiety has no place in the life of the believer. Keep it simple.

## Just a Thought

I have a pastor friend who has often said, "Life is too short for bad coffee and high-maintenance relationships." Tongue in cheek, of course, but usually after one of his congregants has spent too much time in his office, this pastor expresses what many of us fellow pastors have felt from time to time. These pastoral meetings with the *flock* can often be a rehearsal of a litany of complaints and needs. The human tendency to self-absorption can be stifling. The great themes of the kingdom of Heaven, the incarnation, and the resurrection are lost in navel-gazing. Perhaps our much vaunted "personal relationship" with God has become too personal. We reduce the Creator of the universe to a micromanager. He becomes no more than a household deity sought after and dispatched to the resolution of trivialities.

After twenty-five years of local church pastoring, my father had been elected to superintend three hundred churches in southern Ontario. As he was packing up his office, I asked him what he would do differently as a pastor if he had it to do over again. Without a hint of hesitation he answered, "I'd be harder." This is not to say that there aren't genuine concerns needing pastoral consultation and prayer. Rather, it's an admission that pastors, to be kind and/or to affirm their own need to be needed, can unwittingly enable self-absorption. Thus the toleration of the weekly two-hour visit from the underemployed melancholic who loves to be center of attention (plus there's no fee), or the disgruntled spouse whose marriage is in constant uproar. The focus on oneself is ultimately spiritually eviscerating. Prayer can become the language of high maintenance. Heaven rolls its eyes . . .

This is why "give us this day our daily bread" is genius. It expresses a universal human need (food security), acknowledges dependence on a provident father, and leaves secondary (sometimes spurious) wants in the background. What's more, it jibes with "think not what the morrow bringeth . . ." And it's an expression of trust. Prayer morphs from Bob Wiley's "I need, I need, I need" (in the movie *What About Bob)* to "thank you." Gratitude is the sure sign of low maintenance. A thankful spirit has little room for anxiety.

Simplicity

# Window No. 8
# Prayer

### He Sees Us

Thank you, our loving Father,
That you are "the God who sees."
You know our names, our needs,
Our burdens,
Providing for every contingency.
Because you are provident we have freedom
From anxiety.
There is no need to buffer ourselves—we are
Secure, not insecure.
You have given us
Our daily bread today,
And tomorrow, and tomorrow you are
Faithful.
We will fear no evil
For you are with us.
However dark the valley
You walk with us.
Even in death you guide
Us into your eternal presence.
In you O Lord
We put our trust.

## Window No. 9
# Forgiveness

> The highest sacrifice is a broken and contrite heart;
> The highest wisdom is that which is found in the Torah;
> The noblest of all ornaments is modesty;
> And the most beautiful thing that man can do
> is to forgive a wrong.
>
> —RABBI ELEAZAR OF WORMS, 1176–1238

SOMETIMES OPENING A WINDOW can be difficult. The frame, swollen or worn by weather, resists, and a good deal of force is necessary. This is often the way it is with forgiveness. When we pray, "Forgive us our debts, as we forgive (or, have forgiven) our debtors," the words stick in our throats. The conditional aspect, the quid pro quo, seems unfair. Do I *really* have to forgive in order to be forgiven?

The words we use and the meanings we give to them are, of course, critical in understanding and in communication. Our concept of "forgiveness" and of "debt" or "transgression" can powerfully enlighten or distort what Jesus was getting at. So a brief word study in the biblical languages is vital to our hearing him.

In biblical Hebrew there are a number of verbs used to describe the act of forgiveness: *kaphar* ("make atonement"); *macho* ("wipe out"); *kara* ("cover" or "conceal"); *nasa* ("lift up" or "remove"); *abar* ("pass over"); but the most utilized is *salach* ("forgive, pardon"). Interestingly, it is used exclusively of God's forgiveness. Isaiah captured it well (Isa 55:6–7): "Seek the Lord while he may be found; call on him while he is near. Let the wicked forsake their ways and the unrighteous their thoughts; let them turn to the Lord, and he will have mercy on them, and to our God, for he will freely pardon."

And the prophet Jeremiah foresaw a day when there would be divine forgiveness for Israel's rebellious sins:

> No longer will they teach their neighbor, and say to one another "Know the Lord," because they will all know me, from the least of them to the greatest, for I will forgive their wickedness and will remember their sins no more. (Jer 31:34)

> I will cleanse them from all the sin they have committed against me and will forgive all their sins of rebellion against me. (Jer 33:8)

> "In those days, at that time," declares the Lord, "search will be made for Israel's guilt, but there will be none, and for the sins of Judah, but none will be found, for I will forgive the remnant I spare." (Jer 50:20)

As is the case in the Old Testament, there are several words in the New Testament used to denote forgiveness, such as "to wash away, to bestow a favor unconditionally, to dismiss, release, to remit." But two are of special interest: *paresis*, a "passing over" by God of sins committed before the New Covenant came into effect, and *aphiemi*, "to send away," a word Matthew uses here (Matt 6:12).

*Paresis* is used by the apostle Paul in Rom 3:

> 21. But now apart from the law the righteousness of God has been made known to which the Law and the Prophets testify.
>
> 22. This righteousness is given through faith in Jesus Christ to all who believe. There is no difference between Jew and Gentile;

23. for all have sinned and fall short of the glory of God

24. and all are justified freely by his grace through the redemption that came by Christ Jesus.

25. God presented Christ as a sacrifice of atonement, through the shedding of his blood, to be received by faith. He did this to demonstrate his righteousness, because in his *forbearance* he had left the sins committed beforehand *unpunished* [emphasis added].

26. He did it to demonstrate his righteousness at the present time, so as to be just and the one who justifies those who have faith in Jesus.

In his famous speech to the Athenian intellectuals in the book of Acts, Paul used another word (*hyperorao*) to express the same "overlooking" or "disregarding" of sin: "And the times of this ignorance, God *winked at*" (Acts 17:30 KJV; emphasis added).

Paul's understanding of God's "forbearance" (in Greek, *anoche*, meaning "patience") may have reflected Jesus' words: "The servant who knows the master's will and does not get ready or does not do what the master wants will be beaten with many blows. But the one who does not know and does things deserving punishment will be beaten with few blows" (Luke 12:47–48). God has a forgiving heart. He knows that "man is born to trouble as surely as the sparks fly upward" (Job 5:7). And, "he is patient with you not wanting anyone to perish but everyone to come to repentance" (2 Pet 3:9). Indeed, "if our heart condemns us, God is greater than our heart, and knows all things" (1 John 3:20 KJV). Repentance and forgiveness, however, are critical components in restoring the broken relationship between God and his creatures. Our sin must be "sent away" (in Greek, *aphiemi*).

This "sending away" of sin was graphically illustrated by the scapegoat on the Day of Atonement in Israel's desert wanderings. The Lord instructed Moses to confer the sins of Israel onto a goat and send it out to the wilderness, far from the camp, in order to "make atonement" for the people (Lev 16:8, 10, 26). In this way, they were forgiven and cleansed, God's divine wrath was appeased, and the offence completely removed.

So what is being sent away? Jesus says it's our "debts." Then, just after the Prayer, he restates the case by calling the disciples to forgive others' "transgressions" (Matt 6:14–15 KJV). His hearers would have understood debt as a "loan with biting interest" (in Hebrew, *neshekh*). Some commentators see "debts" as *sins of omission*; that is, failure to fulfill God's expectations. The "transgressors" (in Greek, *parabater*) were deliberate in acts of breaking rules, crossing boundaries and rebellion ("sins of commission"). In either case, these sins were to be "sent away."

Forgiveness is not static. It is ongoing. The apostle John, referring to our sinful behavior as believers, said, "The blood of Jesus his Son cleanses us from all sin" (1 John 1:7 KJV). The view here is that of a continuous present: "keeps on cleansing us . . ." So, too, our brother's trespasses against us may seem endless, but we're to forgive "seventy times seven" (Matt 18:22 KJV). This is not to suggest that we enable injurious behavior. No. We deal with the behavior assertively (e.g., leaving that abusive husband and/or reporting him to the authorities) but we do not harbor the injustice. We let it go. We send it away even as we send the abuser away. If we don't, bitterness will take root and destroy our soul. Forgiveness liberates and heals.

To stress the perspective we must have re: forgiveness, Jesus told a story. A man who owed his king "ten thousand bags of gold" (!) begged for more time to pay back the money. The king did better than that—he forgave the entire debt. The forgiven debtor then went out and began to choke someone who owed him "a hundred silver coins" demanding repayment. He refused to show mercy and sent the unfortunate man to prison. The king heard about it and sent him to jail to be tortured (!) until he repaid the huge amount he owed (Matt 18:23–35).

It was just a parable and, as he often did, Jesus employed a bit of hyperbole. But the point was clear: what we owe our heavenly Father far outstrips any debt our neighbor may owe us. When we've been forgiven so much, how can we not forgive the petty debt owed us? And the warning from Jesus: "This is how my heavenly

Father will treat each of you unless you forgive your brother or sister from your heart."

So, if we're not prepared to forgive we'd better stop praying the Lord's Prayer. Close that window. Only repentance and a forgiving spirit will open it again. It's about integrity.

## I Wish We Had a King

On my weekly drives from Jerusalem to southern Lebanon I used to take the Jordan Valley highway. It was a poorly maintained two-lane road with plenty of off-camber curves and narrow, sometimes nonexistent shoulders. From Jerusalem to Jericho one travels down, down, down (Jerusalem's elevation is 2,500 feet above sea level; Jericho's elevation is 800 feet below sea level) through the Judean hills. The transition from Mt. Zion to the Rift Valley is dramatic.

For about eleven months of the year, the Judean wilderness is barren. The hills (or mountains as some call them) blister in desert heat from May to September. October and November usually see more moderate temperatures. Then, from December through March there can be (although not always) rain, accompanied on occasion by weeks of very chilly weather. Sometimes there is snow in Jerusalem. April is amazing. For a few weeks the Judean wasteland is ablaze with a riot of brilliance. It's as though an artist has splashed a canvas with buckets of yellows, reds, blues, violets, and every other color that captures the eyes. Why? Because throughout the winter hundreds of thousands of birds have migrated from Asia to Africa over the land bridge of Israel, dropping exotic seeds from the skies, their excreta providing tailor-made fertilizer. The rains of February and March germinate the millions of seeds and the returning heat of April brings an explosion of flora. It truly is breathtaking. Israelis (who are natural-born environmentalists) flock to the region in droves, taking photos even as they take care to avoid stepping on the fragile beauty. I remember one year when the winter had been unusually wet that the blaze of flowers extended all the way down (1,400 feet below sea level) to the shores of the Dead Sea. It was a wonder to the nation.

Driving that ribbon of asphalt north from Jericho to Tiberias on the Sea of Galilee was not always routine. The curves, valleys (*wadis*), mountains, and place names remained, but the events and traffic volume varied. By "events," I do mean events. A few times over the years on my weekly drive to the Upper Galilee I had to stop at military checkpoints because of suspected terrorist activity. There was a security road bordering the entire length of the highway, constructed of two parallel chain-link fences with a dusty fifty-foot-wide ribbon of sand between them. I would often see a military Jeep towing a harrow throwing up a huge cloud of dust as it prepared an even surface for that night. The point was to detect any footprints the next morning. If evidence of an incursion by terrorists breaching the fence were to appear, every vehicle (including mine) along the highway was stopped and searched.

A major event occurred during Israel's invasion of Lebanon in 1982. I happened to be driving the Jordan Valley road just as Israel mobilized their ground forces. I was suddenly caught in bumper-to-bumper traffic with massive trucks carrying tanks, armored personnel carriers, and huge cannons. The camouflaged netting over these armaments only added to the surreal experience of being the only civilian vehicle in four lines (!) of slow moving might straddling the two-lane highway and narrow shoulders. It took five and a half hours to get from Bet Shean to Qiryat Shemona. As we inched up the slope to Metula, the forest on our left was ablaze with a fire caused by mortar shells launched out of Lebanon.

One other fateful day a small group of Israeli high school students were visiting a lookout over the Jordan Valley just south of the Sea of Galilee. Without warning, a disgruntled Jordanian soldier who had surreptitiously made his way to the base of the lookout opened fire. Some of the students were killed. When news of this tragedy spread, all of Israel was outraged. There were vitriolic calls for revenge. But then in a day or so, everything calmed down. Why? The answer is astonishing.

King Hussein of Jordan, a man widely admired by Israelis, made a secret trip to Israel in order to personally visit the families of the slain students. He took responsibility for the violent actions of the rogue soldier and asked for forgiveness. Struck by his humility and compassion the grieving families forgave. And a potential firestorm was averted.

In the amazement that blanketed Israel following this act of contrition one of our Israeli friends said wistfully, "I wish we had a king."

## Window No. 9
## Prayer

### The Most Beautiful Thing

Your word O Lord, teaches that
We "are born to trouble"—most of it
Self-inflicted.
Our appetites, acquisitions, and accomplishments can
Compromise our relationship with you
And with one another.
We often say "sorry" with our mouths
But don't mean it in our hearts—and we suspect
Others do the same.
And so begins a long story of dark memory and repressed
Resentment.
Help us to be like you—ready to forgive,
Eager to restore relationship.
Help us to turn the other cheek,
To walk in the other's shoes,
Freeing the offender and ourselves
From the toxins of quid pro quo.
As you are forbearing may we be forbearing.
As you are patient may we be patient.
As you forgive may we forgive.
May our long memory be of grace.

## Window No. 10
# Courage

> Happiness depends on being free,
> and freedom depends on being courageous.
>
> —Thucydides, *History of the Peloponnesian War*, fifth century

WHEN JESUS WAS HANGING on the cross, he was assailed by hostile mockers. Matthew records one of the meanest insults: "He saved others . . . but he can't save himself" (Matt 27:42). They got it half right. Yes, he saved others but he *wouldn't* save himself.

His refusal to use his divine power for self-interest went right back to his temptation by Satan after his baptism (Matt 4:1–11). His vision and character as Son of God trumped mere material fame, fortune, and brokered power interests. With scriptural bracing (Deut 6:13,16; Deut 8:3), he resisted the lure of instant gratification and sensational appeals to his Father. His integrity was his defense.

The apostle John described temptation as "all that is in the world, the lust of the flesh, and the lust of the eyes, and the pride of life" (1 John. 2:16 KJV). Appetite is not the issue—hunger is God-given. But it's the overreach ("lust") that is the issue. Temptation is the incitement to go beyond what God intended.

Enjoying things ("flesh"), obtaining things ("eyes"), and accomplishing things ("pride") are common, legitimate human interests. They're implicit in "all that is in the world." It's just that there is much more than that which is available to the senses. For the child of God there is eternity beyond the horizon with its limitless possibilities. "All these things" which the world offers will be "added unto" those who "seek first his kingdom and his righteousness" (Matt 6:33). Enjoying, obtaining, and achieving things must serve the greater interest. Moderation will keep us on track.

But, there's something else about temptation that doesn't readily occur to the casual reader. The word Matthew used was *peirasmos* ("trials"). This was not the temptation to yield to mere lust, but to persecution, spiritual agonies, and perceived abandonment. This was the kind of trial Jesus faced in the Garden of Gethsemane: "My Father if it is possible, may this cup be taken from me" (Matt 26:39b). He would have us pray that the Father will lead us away from such trials. He wouldn't wish them on anyone, although he knew his disciples would face them at every turn in preaching the gospel to all the world. They would be tried by cross and sword.

The bottom line prayer re: temptation/trial is to be delivered (*rhyomai*, meaning "to drag out of danger") from *poneros* (the "evil one"). We're talking *Satan* here, our overrated adversary.

In many religious mythologies over the centuries, *dualism* saw two divinities—one good the other evil, waging war on each other. The outcomes of these conflicts were never certain, and their subject peoples were forever caught in the grip of fear and insecurity. The good divinity had to be worshiped and the evil placated. Sometimes the mercurial nature of both had the people scrambling to provide appropriate sacrifices and liturgies. When you were never sure who the winner might be, you had to cover all the bases.

In Jesus' day, right up to our own, the malevolent one was/is referred to as "Satan" (Hebrew, *adversary*). He was the "accuser" or the "devil" who lay in wait to ambush, "to steal, kill, and destroy" (John 10:10). He was relentless and implacable in his predation.

Unfortunately, he was seen as the obverse of goodness, the dualistic dark side capable of ravaging and dominating whomever and whatever he desired. His power was divine.

But he was/is *not* divine. He is a creature. He is not all-knowing (omniscient), all-powerful (omnipotent), all-present (omnipresent), perfect, or holy. He cannot read our minds nor can he make us do anything. He can guess, seduce, suggest, and manipulate, yet if we resist him he "flees" from us (Jas 4:7)! But, "like a roaring lion seeking whom he may devour" (1 Pet 5:8 KJV), he preys on the weak. Lying is his foot in the door.

Often, the default of well-meaning believers is to blame Satan for their wrong choices. They may not go so far as to declare (à la comedian Flip Wilson) "the devil made me do it!" but they pretty much defer any outcomes to him. It is a *spiritualized* avoidance of accountability. In so doing they give Satan far too much credit. Sadly, a lack of knowledge provides a seedbed for superstition.

The Hebrew root "s-t-n" (there are no vowels) has a basic meaning: "obstruct, oppose." It refers to anyone or anything acting in an adversarial role. In the strange story of the prophet Balaam, the "angel of the Lord" opposed him (s-t-n) in his misguided attempt to curse Israel (Num 22:23–32). In another, the Philistine commanders of King Achish's army who had employed David as a mercenary were nervous about his loyalty and warned that "he will be an adversary" (s-t-n) against them in the heat of the battle (1 Sam 29:4). In the Psalms, David calls on God to appoint an accuser (s-t-n) against his enemies (Ps 109:6).

In the book of Job, a member of the heavenly court acts as a prosecuting attorney and accuser (*ha satan*, "the satan"), but is not represented as chief of a rival dominion or as God's antagonist. Similarly an "accuser" (*ha satan*) in Zech 3:1–2 is seen in a vision, accusing Joshua the high priest, whereupon the Lord rebukes him. Then, in 1 Chr 21:1, we read that "Satan" (proper name this time) incited David to take a census, but in the earlier version of events (2 Sam 24:1), it is the Lord himself who incites the king. Perhaps the chronicler thought in terms of an angelic *prosecutor* delegated to do the will of the Lord. Then there is the "Lucifer" in the KJV translation of the Hebrew *Helel* ("Daystar"), referring to the king of Babylon who thought he would "ascend to heaven" but is about to be "cut down to the ground" (Isa 14:3-23).

The New Testament picks up on the chronicler's proper noun and refers to *Satanas* sometimes also calling him *ho diabolos* ("the obstructor" or "devil"). There are a number of other names used: "tempter" (Matt 4:3; 1 Thess 3:5); "Beelzebul" (Matt 12:24); "enemy" (Matt 13:39); "evil one" (Matt 6:13; 13:19,38; 1 John 2:13,14; 3:12); "Belial" (2 Cor 6:15); "enemy" (1 Pet 5:8); "dragon" (Rev 12:3); "father of lies" (John 8:44); "murderer" (John 8:44); and "sinner" (1 John. 3:8 KJV). The most commonly used are "Satan" or "devil"—the very one who tried to take Jesus down (Matt 4:1-11).

In the book of Revelation, the apostle John has a vision of a war in heaven between "Michael and his angels" and "the dragon [Satan] and his angels" (Rev 12:7-12). Apocalyptic literature by definition is not a historical record, but a kaleidoscopic overload of visions, symbols, color, and mystery. Trying to decipher and reduce it to systematic doctrine or dogma is a nonstarter. Nevertheless, it provides a powerful stimulus for thought and eschatological anticipation. John's vision gives no explanation as to how or why Satan and his "angels" (read *demons*) are in heaven, nor the reason for the war. It simply makes the point that Satan is "the deceiver of the whole world" (Rev 12:9) and has been "thrown down to the earth" where he dwells "in great wrath because he knows his time is short" (Rev 12:12 KJV)! He is doomed (see Rev 20), but his death throes will cause untold collateral damage. The "prince of the power of the air" (Eph 2:2 KJV) will not easily exit the stage but he *will* exit.

When the seventy-two newly minted disciples returned from their "boot camp" mission they were chuffed by their mastery over evil spirits (Luke 10:17). Rather than enthuse with them, Jesus basically said, "Good for you fellas, but keep things in perspective. You cast out a few demons whereas I saw Satan fall like lightning from heaven. Just be glad your names are written in heaven" (Luke 10:18-20). Jesus was unintimidated: "The prince of the world is coming. He has no hold over me" (John 14:30). The writer to the

Hebrews put it this way: "Since the children have flesh and blood, he too shared in their humanity so that by his death he might break the power of him who holds the power of death—that is, the devil" (Heb 2:14). Courageously he took on the weight of the cross and the agonies of death in order to "destroy the works of the devil" (1 John 3:8 KJV).

Jesus knew that the battle would be tough for his disciples. He knew that even as Satan had tried to do with Peter he would attempt to "sift each of you as wheat" (Luke 22:31). Christian faith and ministry would cast them into the arena of Satan's last battle and there would be casualties. So Jesus with a tender heart taught them to pray "deliver us from the evil one." Be faithful. Be strong. Be courageous. Jesus has your back. There's nothing to fear. Let the light shine in.

## Theresa

It was a hot and muggy evening in Lilongwe, Malawi when I first met Theresa Malila. The church was poorly lit, with swarms of hummingbird-sized mosquitoes preying on a congregation of forty. Kathy and I had begun our ministry to orphans and widows eighteen months previously. It was now nearing 2002. That first year and a half had seen us starting from scratch in South Africa and Zimbabwe and we'd gained experience and a degree of traction in that formative time. Now we were beginning our outreach to other African countries. Malawi, the fourth poorest country in the world, was first on our radar.

It may have been the heat, the mosquitoes, the low wattage lighting, all in combination with jet lag, but regardless, I was feeling a bit down that night. Mind you, when I spoke I did so (as always) as though I were speaking to a thousand. The biblical call to righteousness and justice and its practical application to at-risk orphans and widows suffering the ravages of HIV and AIDS was my message. At the close of the service a well-dressed woman, accompanied by two young adults, approached me. There were tears in her eyes.

"Hello Pastor, my name is Theresa Malila, and these are two of my children—Keta and Kiliko. You have touched my heart tonight."

"In what way?" I asked.

"The Lord has been speaking to me about orphans and widows dying of HIV and AIDS. He's calling me to quit my job with government social services and commit full-time to caring for these at risk victims of this horrible disease. It's a scary prospect. I'd be starting with nothing."

"So, what would you like to do?"

"I do not know. Maybe show them somebody cares."

"That would be a good name for your ministry."

"What?"

"You know—'Somebody Cares.' It has a good ring to it."

"Yes. It does have a good sound. Would you pray with me, Pastor? I believe we have the same vision."

The four of us joined hands and I prayed. As I left the church a few minutes later I had no idea that I'd experienced a divine moment that would powerfully impact Malawi. I had just prayed with a saint, who, like another Theresa in India would one day be called "Mother Theresa." Years later, the Tear Fund out of the UK would designate Theresa Malila to be one of the one hundred most influential unknown women in the world.

Over the next couple of years Kathy and I did a lot of exploratory work in Malawi, Zimbabwe, Mozambique, Zambia, and South Africa. In all of these countries I spoke to gatherings of pastors and Christian leaders about the biblical core values of righteousness and justice and its application in caring for orphans and widows victimized by HIV and AIDS. My message was not always well received. The common comment, usually spoken with a tone, was, "Those people are only getting what they deserve. AIDS is punishment from God for immorality." This harsh judgment echoed the attitude of African culture in general. Stigma and discrimination ruled. Indeed, anyone who attempted to stem the tide of infections via social justice efforts (both secular and religious) was seen as endorsing sexual promiscuity. To battle HIV and AIDS, one had to swim against the stream. It took vision, commitment, and courage to act with this kind of countercultural compassion.

I was speaking to two thousand pastors at a mission station outside Kisumu, Kenya, a couple of years after first meeting Theresa. (Our conversation that night in Malawi had all but escaped my memory.) One of my senior staff members had booked a woman to be a speaker at this large conference. He had seen a video of her addressing a group of pastors in Lilongwe and thought she would be a great addition to this Kenyan conference. When she spoke, the pastors were riveted. Not only were they not used to hearing a woman preacher but they were blown away by her content and powerful delivery. During the lunch break we sat across the table from each other.

She looked at me shyly and said, "You don't remember me do you pastor?"

"No. Sorry. I don't."

"Maybe you remember speaking at that church in Lilongwe two years ago? And me and my kids talking to you afterwards?"

In a flash I remembered. "You're Theresa!"

"Malila." She finished my sentence.

"Why didn't I remember your name when you were introduced to speak this morning? I must be getting old."

"No problem. You only heard my name once—two years ago. You're forgiven," she laughed. "And you should know that after our prayer that night I quit my government job and started a ministry to dying orphans and widows."

"What do you call it?"

"Somebody Cares," she said with a smile. "You named it, remember?"

Six months later Kathy and I joined Theresa on one of her ministry visits to a village outside of Lilongwe. Even though she had been at it for two years her ministry kit was less than basic: a Bible and a small bottle of oil. Her method was equally humble: assess the situation, provide water for the patient, shift him or her in their prone position, then read a passage of Scripture in the presence of the dying orphan or widow (usually with several villagers present), anoint them with oil, and pray. We watched her in action as we walked the dusty paths from *rondavel* to *rondavel* (round mud huts with grass roofs). It seemed every little home had someone in distress, but they saw Theresa as a visiting angel. Their eyes would light up in her presence. Hers was the healing power of hope in Jesus' name.

Even though our ministry was also young, I decided we would come alongside Somebody Cares both in mobilizing pastors and churches in Malawi and in providing financial support. She was a true champion, someone whose ministry would stand the test of time.

At the time of writing (over twenty years later), Theresa and Somebody Cares have stood strong. She has faced (especially in the early years when she was walking alone from village to village) everything from sexual harassment to vilification by pastors and chiefs. She has often referred to the spiritual warfare she has endured. But her integrity is intact. Today, Somebody Cares is engaged with vulnerable orphans and widows in thousands of homes. Theresa has become "a national treasure." Her vision, commitment, and courage are unassailable. Neither hardship nor the *evil one* has been able to break her godly resolve.

## Window No. 10
## Prayer

### A Spiritual Backbone

Almighty God in whom
We put our trust,
Deliver us, we pray, from the evil one,
The father of lies
Whose practice is to steal, kill, and destroy.
He tempts, intimidates, manipulates,
Seduces...
Our feeble hearts his prey.
Yet, O Lord, we are yours
Not his.
You have promised that "no evil
Shall befall" us,
That you will give your angels
"Charge over us,"
That you will "deliver us"
As we dwell "in the secret place."
Father, we are weak
But you are strong.
Whatever the challenge,
Whatever the adversity
Or adversary,
We pray that you will be our strong tower,
Our fortress in time of need.

Postscript
# David's Prayer

AT THE BEGINNING OF this book I referred to Jesus saying the kingdom of Heaven belongs to "the poor in spirit." This may be the pivot point of the entire Sermon on the Mount. It strikes most of us as counterintuitive in that we tend to think heaven is for those who deserve it, that our "good works" earn us entry. Yet, there are several instances in the biblical record not only of the people of Israel but also prominent leaders who confess their sins and plead for God's forgiveness. Perhaps the most poignant of all is David's prayer in Ps 51. It's a prayer of total contrition from a heart overwhelmed with guilt, crushed and broken by shame. If anyone in Israel was poor in spirit at that point in history, it was the king (vv. 16–17).

The sordid story in 2 Samuel, chapters 11 and 12, pulls no punches. It's a tale no preacher wants to reference in a sermon. It's about adultery, deception, murder, and secrecy—a secret David hid for upwards of a year. But it's also about huge guilt, loss of sleep, and agonies of soul: "When I kept silence, my bones waxed old through my roaring all the day long. For day and night Thy hand was heavy upon me: my moisture is turned into the drought of summer" (Ps 32:3–4 KJV).

So how can a man with such a wretched, spiritually impoverished heart be the same man whom the prophet Samuel referred to as someone "after God's own heart"? (1 Sam 13:14). Was not David a prime example of youthful innocence devolving to adult arrogance, of a pure heart blemished by power, predating by more than two millennia Lord Acton's cynical observation that "power corrupts, and absolute power corrupts absolutely"?[1] How could he even presume to approach the holy God in prayer?

Like any of us when we've behaved badly, David would have expected rebuke and rejection both from those he'd sinned against (including a disgusted public) and perhaps God himself. But the "smoking flax" and the "bruised reed" (Isa 42:3) enabled him to pray "according to thy lovingkindness . . . the multitude of thy tender mercies blot out my transgressions" (Ps 51:1 KJV). He was down but not out. There was yet a whisper of smoke from his crushed soul.

David's prayer is highly emotive and desperately urgent. It gushes from his heart. As such, it is not to be studied as a template for prayer. Rather it is an example of the passion of regret. It's as though a soul teeters on the edge of a precipice. David is in need of acute divine intervention. It is comprised of seventeen petitions and three promises (Ps 51):

1. Have mercy on me (1a)

2. Blot out my transgressions (1c)

3. Wash away all my iniquity (2a)

4. Cleanse me from my sin (2b)

5. Cleanse me with hyssop (7a)

6. Wash me (7b)

7. Hide your face from my sins (9a)

8. Blot out all my iniquity (9b)

9. Create in me a pure heart (10a)

10. Renew a steadfast spirit within me (10b)

11. Do not cast me from your presence (11a)

---

1. John Dalberg-Acton, "Letter to Bishop Mandell Creighton," in *Life and Letters of Mandell Creighton*, edited by Louise Creighton (London: Longmans, Green and Co., 1905).

12. Do not take your Holy Spirit from me (11b)
13. Restore to me the joy of your salvation (12a)
14. Grant me a willing spirit (12b)
15. Save me from blood guilt (14a)
16. Open my lips (15a)
17. Build up the walls of Jerusalem (18b)
18. I will teach transgressors your ways (13a)
19. I will sing of your righteousness (14b)
20. I will declare your praise (15b)

The fact that David even presumed to pray this prayer may be evidence that he had read God's word to Moses when he said, "The Lord, the Lord, the compassionate and gracious God, slow to anger, abounding in love and faithfulness, maintaining love to thousands, and forgiving wickedness, rebellion and sin. Yet he does not leave the guilty unpunished; he punishes the children and their children for the sins of the parents to the third and fourth generation" (Exod 34:6–7). The *guilty* are those who have not confessed and repented. David wanted to be sure to be one of the forgiven. But the enormity of his sins was such that he needed to cast himself upon the mercy and compassion (also seen as *loving-kindness*), grace, and faithfulness of God.

God's revelation to Moses had included those four qualities without which David and all sinners had no hope. His compassion (in Hebrew, *racha*) was the deep love and mercy of a father, expressed tenderly to his children; his grace (*chen*) was the heartfelt response from a superior to an inferior who had no real claim for gracious treatment; his loving-kindness (*chesed*) was love and truth in action, freely rescuing and delivering the lost; and his faithfulness (*emet*), which also means "truth," underscored his dependability, the certainty that he would be true to his nature. It was upon these immutable foundation stones that David built his hope that God would forgive (*nasa*, "to lift up, bear") his sins of adultery, murder and deception.

## Postscript

David's first petition is a cry from the heart: "Have mercy on me, O God." Indeed this could be called the title of the prayer. Everything that follows is predicated on mercy. David was truly impoverished spiritually and emotionally. There is no hint of self-confidence, triumphalism, or rationalism in his words. He was a supplicant. Then, over the next five petitions he calls on God to blot out his transgressions, wash away his iniquity, and cleanse him from sin. The nuances of these three verbs and three nouns are lost in our twenty-first-century verbal and spiritual vocabulary, but they provide fascinating insight into how David and the Israelites of his day understood their relationship with the God of Abraham, Isaac, and Jacob.

First of all the verbs: "blot . . . wash . . . cleanse." In Isa 44:22 (KJV) we read: "I have blotted out, as a thick cloud, thy transgressions, and as a cloud, thy sins." The concept is that of a written record being wiped away. But a nuance that can be missed is that God blots out transgressions for *his own sake*. If he doesn't wipe out the record, his justice will require punishment. David wants that requirement to be removed. Then there is the plea for God to "wash" all David's iniquity away. The imagery here is that of the fuller who launders by way of treading, kneading, and beating away any contamination in cold water. (This is a method I've seen in present day India and Sri Lanka.) David wants to be clean regardless of the suffering the process may require. Thirdly, he asks for cleansing. This means purity equal to the stringent demands of Israel's sacrificial system. David wants to be ritually clean, declared free of any blemish and fit for liturgical protocols. And he knows that only God can cleanse.

The nuances of the three nouns for sin are equally fascinating: "transgression . . . iniquity . . . sin." David sees himself as a rebel ("transgression" in Hebrew is *peshah*), "twisted" and "bent" on the inside (*ava* "iniquity"), and someone who has "missed the mark" (*chita*, "sin"). He's ready to be *laundered* from his rebellious behavior and sin that are products of his essentially twisted nature. His actions on the outside reflect the *thick cloud* of rottenness on the inside. This jibes with the Lord's word to Samuel: "For the Lord seeth not as man seeth; for man looketh on the outward appearance but the Lord looketh on the heart" (1 Sam 16:7 KJV). Darkness resides within, collateral damage without.

The first eight petitions all have to do with David's remorse for his adultery with Bathsheba, his murder of her husband Uriah, and his year-long cover-up of this horrible behavior. These sins are in the past, but are ever-present. He needs to be forgiven, freed from the remorseless attacks of conscience, and healed from the debilitating disease of his moral failures. But he needs more than a cleansing confessional break with the past. He needs a new beginning. Indeed, he needs to be made new. What's more, he needs to *act* new, which is what true repentance means.

David's "twisted" and "bent" heart needs to be recreated. And so he petitions the Lord to "create in me a pure heart" (petition 9). Without this inner healing, he will continue in his iniquity and will be without hope. The prophet Isaiah captured the hopelessness and domino effect of unredeemed souls when he wrote (Isa 59 KJV),

> 12. For our transgressions are multiplied before thee and our sins testify against us: for our transgressions are with us; and as for our iniquities we know them;
>
> 13. In transgressing and lying against the Lord, and departing from our God, speaking oppression and revolt, conceiving and uttering from the heart words of falsehood.
>
> 14. And judgment is turned away backwards and justice standeth afar off: for truth is fallen in the street, and equity cannot enter,
>
> 15a. Yea truth faileth . . .

And when truth fails all else fails with it.

So when David asks for the renewal of "a steadfast spirit" (petition 10), he is asking for a strong and dependable (in Hebrew, *firm*) inner resolve that will eschew deceit. In modern Hebrew, one uses the same word translated "steadfast" in the affirmative *nachon*, or "yes." It has the nuance of the biblical "yea" and "amen,"

## POSTSCRIPT

which essentially denotes a faithful yes. You can depend on someone with a steadfast spirit. They will not lie.

In petitions 11 and 12 he may be thinking of his predecessor King Saul—a mighty man anointed with the Spirit, standing head and shoulders above the nation, who fell ignominiously from God's favor. "The Spirit of the Lord departed from Saul" (1 Sam 16:14) are some of the saddest words in the Bible. Please, don't let me be like him, David pleads. I want to be joyful again, exulting in your salvation (petition 13). I want to be malleable in your hands (petition 14), the "bloods" (plural in Hebrew) of my past eclipsed by open lips and mouth singing your praise (petitions 15 and 16). I want to teach your ways to transgressors, sing of your righteousness with a *rising cry* (Hebrew), and *conspicuously* (Hebrew nuance) declare your praise (Ps 51:13–15). I want you, O Lord, to delight in my brokenness and contrition. My heart seeks your heart. Full stop.

Now, back to work. We need to finish those new walls around Jerusalem (Ps 51:18b) (also see Josephus *Antiquities of the Jews* 7:3, 20). There is more than my personal needs to be met. I must fulfill my kingly duties as you have anointed me to do . . .

\* \* \*

I have included this postscript to encourage you, the reader. None of us may be guilty as David of such heinous sins, but we all have sinned secretly and have borne the weight of conscience. When we open the windows of our souls light is shed on those sins and we sometimes cover them quickly. Prayer exposes our moral nakedness. So here's a word from the Bible: "And hereby we know that we are of the truth and shall assure our hearts before him. For if our heart condemns us, God is greater than our heart, and knoweth all things" (1 John 3:19–20 KJV).

Remember these words. God knows you. He knows the circumstances of your upbringing. He knows the dark moments of your life's journey. He sees the big picture. You are part of it. There will be an end game where you will hear "Well done, good and faithful servant, enter thou into the joy of thy Lord." The Lord will never despise a broken and a contrite heart. You can count on it.

## Prayer

The grace of the Lord Jesus Christ,
And the love of God,
And the communion of the Holy spirit,
Be with you all.
Amen.

Printed in the USA
CPSIA information can be obtained
at www.ICGtesting.com
LVHW010157240324
775246LV00002B/6